Girl on Top

Girl on Top

Your Guide to
Turning Dating Rules
into Career Success

Nicole Williams

CENTER
STREET.

New York   Boston   Nashville

Center Street
Hachette Book Group
237 Park Avenue
New York, NY 10017

www.centerstreet.com

Center Street is a division of Hachette Book Group, Inc.
The Center Street name and logo are trademarks of Hachette Book Group, Inc.

Printed in the United States of America

First Edition: October 2009
10 9 8 7 6 5 4 3 2

Library of Congress Cataloging-in-Publication Data

Williams, Nicole
   Girl on top : your guide to turning dating rules into career success/
Nicole Williams—1st ed.
      p.   cm.
   ISBN 978-1-59995-192-8
   1. Women—Employment—Psychological aspects.   2. Achievement motivation
in women.   3. Attitude (Psychology)   4. Self-actualization (Psychology)
5. Success—Psychological aspects.   6. Women—Vocational guidance.   I. Title.

HD6053.W48 2009
650.1082—dc22   2009015411

Book design by Laurie Neff

Michael Loeb, thank you for betting on this jockey.

Acknowledgments

No girl gets on top without riding the talent, inspiration, and sheer effort of a mountain of supporters. This book simply wouldn't have been possible without the following: My agent, Rebecca Oliver, for coming up with such a fitting title (for someone with an aversion to "balls" you really pulled out a provocative one). To my editor, Michelle Rapkin, for not being able to live without it and publisher, Harry Helm, for believing in its potential. To my business partners: Michael Loeb, my fellow "Working Girl" (thank you for raising the bridge for this little girl from Ajax); Rich Vogel, for putting on your girl voice, explaining, on way too many occasions, the concept of supply and demand, and for making it real in our business; and Robert Imershein for sprinkling your inspiration, honor, and brain power all over WORKS. To Jennifer Bedell for the fact that the aforementioned partners would never be at any of my meetings on time without you. I will never forget the day you called to ask for the package and know without you it would not have gotten into the right hands. I'm forever grateful. Nahila Chianale, for making me look, and more important, feel like I can take on the world. Maggie Bock for not only ensuring the checks get cashed but for cheering me on behind the scenes.

To the WORKS team: Kimmy Scotti this book—from concept to

cover—wouldn't have become real without you. You make every-thing easier and so much more fun. Thank you for your loyalty and friendship. Stephanie Reese and Michelle Hainer, for driving it to the finish line with your amazing and never-ending ideas, voice, and edits. Rachel Barrett, for lending me the Chico and for picking up what I'm putting down. Andrew Segoshi, Ed McCabe, Andrew Slutsky, and Jack Lennon, for adding some testosterone to the team and for allowing me to harass you. Jon Jenson, for pushing out 500 words on the train ride, making sure someone actually reads all this shit, and giving me first taste of child labor (thanks Zoe!). And a special thank you to all the WORKS freelance writers who contribute to our website each and every day.

A heartfelt thanks to all my friends and family: My mom, Linda Williams, for landing such a shitty job and inspiring this whole career thing. My beloved nana Doris Smith, my gramps Ernie Smith and nana Eileen Williams. My brother, Shane, and his wife, Melanie, thank you for supplying me with an ever-waiting home. My two Jennifers—Little and Hannay—always in my heart. Maria Eftimiades, I have never met anyone more brave or generous. Heller, Munkton says it all. Terry Leiweke for ordering me to put your bag in the overhead and introducing me to your wife, Shelley. Shelley for downing bottles of rose, welcoming me to your home and sharing your family. Jen Leiweke for being like the sister I've always longed for. Pam Fryman for inspiring me with your talent and spirit. Susan Hamilton, Maeve Raeddle, and Pat Duffy, my because-of-dogs friends till the end. The Vancouver cheering squad: Edna (Roxy Roller) Zurbuchen, Con Buckley, Praveen Varshney, Paul Grehan.

Contents

Introduction

Let's go back. It's March 27, 2004. I know the day, the exact day, because I was at the wedding of one of my best friends. Sitting in a front pew (her sister was her only bridesmaid), absorbing the vows (self-written), holding the hand of my husband (uncharacteristically clammy), I decided I was leaving (not the church . . . my marriage).

There were, of course, the requisite dastardly, excruciating, heartbreaking months in between, but on one special day, sick and tired of my distress, a friend came by my new apartment with a basket of get-out-of-your-funk goodies. It was filled to the brim with everything from chocolate and erotic porn to a library of dating books, and that night, as I jumped into my big, lonely bed and strategically chose *The Rules* over the vibrator, my life changed.

Page after page I devoured the words that were meant for my love life, and I was struck with one shining beacon of discovery . . . pure career genius.

Here's the thing: I'm a career manager so I do tend to look at the world through the lens of work. Thanks to my mother who, working for a paint and chemical manufacturer, lived a special kind of hell, I grew up with the desire to actually spend my days doing something I enjoyed. As a kid, I would drive people to drink with questions of, "How did you know you wanted to be a doctor?" "Where did you learn that?" and "How much do you get paid?" I was a one-woman career investigative team terrified of hating my job (which really means hating your life), and I ultimately parlayed that fear into a career management brand called WORKS.

But get this: Even before I read and reread *The Rules,* I was, and still am, a good dater. The whole concept of "playing hard to get" is as natural to me as breathing. Love dating or hate it: We know it. We need it. We do it. In my business I've been forever trying to convince women that working for less than industry standard is going to kill their career but now I have a context to wrap it around— *Don't give away the milk for free.*

After that fateful night in bed, I took a cruise through the bookstore and online and found the top twenty classic dating rules and then turned them into career strategies. Treat him mean to keep him keen; don't tell him you want a kid on the first date (or interview); don't expect to change him . . . I didn't make this shit up, but I promise I've found the key to applying it to your career in a way that will change your life.

So, the most important question and the whole reason I'm so adamant you read this introduction is: **Who is the HE?** *He* is your boss, your assistant, your client, your vendor. Anyone and everyone you do business with. And just like our tendency is to throw out the rule book and call, and call, and call, and call the super hot dude you can't help but imagine is "the one," you're going to come across the job, the boss, the client you can't imagine yourself living without, and it's exactly here where you need to play the game. Finding, catching, and building a relationship with a beau simply isn't so different from finding, catching, and building a relationship with a boss. We're human, instinctive, and the way we want what we can't have is the same whether we're in the bedroom . . . or the boardroom.

And for those of you who think you're above playing games in love or in career, good for you—have fun in the mailroom and put this book down. I've heard it all before. This isn't intended to be a Pulitzer Prize–winning work of nonfiction—it's an easy-to-get-your-head-around way of thinking about your job, in a language that we're already familiar with, in a context that makes the mind-numbingly boring theory of career a little more fun.

Dating rules turned career strategies . . . everything you need to be the Girl on Top!

Chapter 1

Follow Your Heart

I've been having a love affair for the past seven years. On some days this love of mine seriously drives me to drink but I never seem to tire of it. It inspires me to be bigger and better than I really am. It's broken my heart and I've felt utter disappointment, but I never want to leave. It's simultaneously exhausting and exhilarating. It continually exposes me to brilliant, outrageous, and engaging people and circumstances. And for good or for bad, it's always waiting.

My true love . . . my career.

Having grown up watching my mom hate her job, I have an admittedly obsessive drive to love what I do (and by extension help others get there, too). And while on some days I question whether I'm a wee bit codependent, I never, ever doubt the power of following your heart.

Finding the Love of Your Life

It's the hands-down, number one question I'm asked:

How do I find a career I love?

It comes from women new to the game, those slogging it out for way too many years in the wrong career, or even those who are relatively satisfied but wondering if there might be something more.

Some people search their whole lives and never find a career they love, some fall into love on day one and are committed for life, and still others fall in love over and over again. I've come to believe that just like in our relationships, loving your career has a lot to do with expectations—ultimately you get the love (and the career) you think you deserve. The same friend who has yet to find a man worthy of her affections is in and out of jobs as frequently as you apply gloss. I meet women who won't settle for anything less than rapturous, enduring, passion for their job and others who take a more utilitarian, nine-to-five approach, working simply because they need to pay the bills (and have a little left over for Blahniks) and want to hit the bar by six.

I remember telling my beloved gramps that I was leaving a "stable" [solid income, 401(k), government-funded, management position] to follow my passion, and he seriously thought I was out of my mind. Having lived through a war and the Great Depression and having raised kids as an immigrant working two jobs, for him the whole concept of "loving" a job was downright ludicrous.

You can sit wherever you want on the love-your-job spectrum, but please know that at the end of the day (which in the majority of cases is somewhere between eight and twelve hours), you're spending 70 percent of your waking life working and that's simply too much life to waste wishing the hours away. What's ludicrous from my perch is sitting around, wasting your potential, and never experiencing or sharing the love. If you haven't found the love of your life or if you're still considering other options, here are some places to look.

An arranged marriage

Your mom's a doctor. Your mom's dad is a doctor. His father was a doctor. Not necessarily a bad thing to consider a hand-me-down career with an already established client list and sign on the door. Your passion may very well be found in the genes.

Love at first sight

It's hard to believe but some people come out of the womb knowing they were meant to be a photographer . . . chef . . . florist. This "knowing" is generally some combination of observation (that looks fun) and instinct (that flower would be perfect right . . . there). Take a look around. The love of your life may be right in front of your eyes.

Play the field

The downright best way to increase your odds is by getting out there and exploring your options. I meet a lot of women who think (a) their dream career will magically appear without any effort (it won't), and (b) their first choice is the best and only option (it's not).

Same way you wouldn't expect to marry the first and only guy you ever dated, your long-term career relationship isn't likely to come on the first go-round. Following in my mom's paint factory footsteps when I was in college, I realized somewhere between mind-numbingly stacking paint cans on a skid and checking out the *Playboy* centerfolds in the staff lunch room that sometimes you have to experience the wrong relationship to know what you're looking for in the right one. Sometimes we need exposure to a lot of the wrong options before we land on the right one. Don't be afraid to play the career field. Just remember that—no different than being labeled "easy" in the dating pool—your reputation is everything when it comes to building your career. Feel free to try different jobs on for size in order to find your fit, but keep in mind that at the end of the day you need to stick around long enough to deliver. No one likes a tease.

Still Can't Decide?

I'm all about keeping the cooks out of the kitchen, especially as you're exploring your options (everyone will have an opinion) but there does come a point when a little outside perspective is necessary. If you haven't decided if this is the "one" or have multiple options to consider, it's time to take this new love of yours out on the town. Over drinks or dinner, introduce your peeps to the varying options and ask for their opinion. Don't underestimate how well your friends and family know you and how helpful an outside objective perspective can be. Their insight may be invaluable.

Just be wary of the naysayer. This is a true story. Right after I got engaged, I was walking down the street with the last of our still-single friends and told her the good news. She literally dropped to her knees in the street and started crying, "What about me?" Nothing's more threatening to the lonely, job-hater than the woman who has just gotten her hands on a job she loves.

Note to Self: Desperation Reeks

Unfortunately, as much as you want to find the love of your career, sometimes you need to relax and let it find *you*. Do all that I've suggested, and then open yourself up to the possibilities. The more desperate you are to find "the one," the more likely you are to repel it. Desperation has this nasty way of not only making you blind to what's right there in front of you, but pushing away the very thing you desire most.

Phases of Love

As with any kind of love affair, your career development evolves in three distinct phases, each offering different opportunities and challenges.

Phase one: Courting

The whole point of courtship is to explore your options, feel out if there is interest, and decide if you want to take it to the next level.

This is the one stage in the career exploration process that women move through too quickly. Finding a career you love is all about laying a solid foundation, and frankly, it can take some time. Desperate to not be alone (unemployed), way too many women rush into a commitment (ignoring all the warning signs) with the wrong company and a year later they're back on the streets.

Opportunities: You're not committed, so at this stage it's all about playing the field and exploring fit. This is the perfect time to dig deep and do your research. You have more power than you'd imagine being on the choosing side of the equation. Keep in mind most people are more than willing (delighted even) to talk about themselves, so start chatting them up—you never know where it's going to lead.

Challenges: They all look delicious, so how do you pick just one? Don't be paralyzed by the fear of choosing poorly. Like I mentioned above, the wrong career path very often leads to the right one. At some point you need to lay it down and make a choice. Remember: Nothing has to last forever.

Phase two: Dating

At this point an offer has been made, and the same way you would not be amused if your beau was actively looking for other, hotter options, your current employer expects you to have your eye on his prize. This does not suggest, though, that you can't keep your eyes peeled for other, more interesting options—you can look (go online and see what's available, have conversations over coffee) but don't touch (accept an offer) unless you're truly willing to risk a breakup.

Opportunities: Once you've moved into the exclusive phase of your relationship, it's time to build a more intimate understanding of you as a professional and your industry or employer as a partner. Assess the day-to-day, real-world fit.

Challenges: For months now you've been feeling that something's not right, but the thought of entering a new relationship is more than you can bear. The biggest mistake I see women make is to stay too long in the wrong job or career because they're afraid not only of the work involved in changing positions, but with the unrealistic fear that there's nothing better out there. Don't wait too long to cut your losses if this isn't "the one."

Phase three: Marriage/Long-Term Commitment

You're in. You've finally got that ring on your finger (the title, the raise, or the corner office you've been waiting for), and it's bigger, shinier, and more flauntable than you ever imagined. Though it feels like smooth sailing from here on out, now's the time for consistent checking and balancing.

Opportunities: You're officially in it for the long haul. You've built up enough loyalty, respect, and mutual understanding that you're stable enough to take risks, push your limits, and grow into new talents. You have an established reputation, and at this phase you can relax a little and let them do some of the work.

Challenges: There are two big potential obstacles to this phase of your relationship: (1) you take it for granted, and (2) you've lost the thrill and it loses its appeal. You need to realize not

every day is a bed of roses—even in the career of your life—
but that doesn't necessarily mean it's time to cut and run. Bring
the passion back with communication, taking risks, and re-
membering what made you fall in love in the first place.

Bring Back the Love

It can happen to the best of relationships. Six weeks, six months, six
years down the road, the passion is gone and we find ourselves grip-
ing: "I fell in love with this?" For me it happens at least once a year,
usually when I'm jetlagged, brain-dead, and ready for a drink. I find
myself second-guessing my commitment and asking, "Is this really
how I want to spend the rest of my life?" That's when I know I need
to bring back the love.

Using the same formulas for spicing up your love life, you can
rekindle the passion for your work and actually start falling in love
with your job all over again.

Go back to the way things were

It's inevitable that the thing you initially loved most about your job
is what ends up being the thing you hate. So you wanted autonomy—
well you got it . . . and now you can't motivate yourself to get the
work done. Or you loved the responsibility . . . but now you've got
so much to do you can't breathe. We get so caught up in the day-to-
day business that we forget why we took this on, and who and what
about it is meaningful. Admit that you can't do this all on your own,
ask for help where you need it, and delegate what you're simply not

that great at, and the layers will peel back to reveal what it was that enticed you about this role in the first place.

Make time for each other

When you're so busy flying from task to task that you don't take the time to enjoy what you do, the flame is bound to fizzle. Steal moments of quiet time with the door closed or headphones on (rent a room if you must) so you can really focus. Forget multitasking—concentrate on crossing off one item from your to-do list at a time, and give it your full attention so you can crank out your best work.

Take a reality check

Just like we catch ourselves fantasizing about the hot lifeguard or the strapping fireman in uniform, we have a tendency to wonder if we'd be happier with a different job. What you wouldn't give for a more flexible schedule, better benefits, an office with a no-ass policy . . . The reality is that everyone doesn't like *something* about her job (except for those who haven't been there long enough for the new-love glow to wear off). Talk with others in your industry at different companies, and you'll probably discover you don't have it as bad as you thought. Take comfort in their anguish (secretly, of course) and be grateful for the positive aspects of your position. The truth is the grass *is* always greener no matter where you stand, but you can at least switch up your vantage point. Find an opportunity to challenge yourself, to learn about a different aspect of the business, or to give up the "boss" title for a day—and bring the passion back with a newfound appreciation.

Get yours

Give, give, give. When you're in constant "give mode," burnout comes on full speed. If your career feels like a one-way street, take stock of what you're getting out of the hours you're slogging. You're learning a ton, your skills are improving, you can afford the rent, and you actually like a few of your colleagues. If you're still feeling cheated, make sure your boss is aware of how you'd prefer to be rewarded for your hard work. (Do you want recognition? To be included in more meetings? A bonus?) Name your need. Just be sure to frame it in terms of all you're giving in order to be so deserving (demonstration and examples work wonders). The worst they can say is "no," which every smart girl knows just means "not now."

Loving Yourself

My mom has taught me a lot about what I want, and what I don't want, out of life, but hands down the most invaluable lesson she's shared with me (after quitting that shitty job) is that you can't expect someone to love you if you don't love yourself. I'm totally aware of how incredibly clichéd this sounds, but its application to your career is profound. You and you alone are your biggest career asset and you need to nurture, protect, and invest in yourself with a vengeance. You need to hone and trust your instincts. You need to have standards and never settle for less than what you deserve. If you don't love you—protect you, promote you, invest in you—your career won't give you anything back.

Chapter 2

Treat Him Mean, Keep Him Keen

I t's not an especially difficult concept to wrap our head around, but with a new love on the horizon, we think by virtue of being all sweetness and light, we're as good as hitched. That is, of course, until we've bent over backward, logged hundreds of hours in front of ESPN, and uttered those three little words, only to find ourselves kicked to the curb.

The equation goes something like this. When something (or someone) is nice, it becomes easy. And things that are easy just don't feel as valuable as those that aren't. If you want a guy to desire, fight for, and respect you, there is one simple strategy: Treat him mean to keep him keen.

This principle is as true in courting success as it is in courting love. Just like we gain leverage in love when we have the guts enough to stand up for ourselves, are confident enough to have an opinion, and value ourselves enough to say no to the bullshit—the same holds true at the office.

I honestly believe there is a very critical point in all of our careers when we accept that not everyone is going to agree with us, or get this . . . even like us. That being a leader means making hard and even unpopular choices. That improvement comes with change, and change is never comfortable—especially for the slackers who will be busting you for not being "nice." That we are going to need to say no, reprimand, or even fire, for lack of performance. In other words: We need to be MEAN!

Like Versus Respect

"Mean" is a tough word to digest and can be difficult to wrap your head around. I'm not talking about malice or the kind of whimsical disagreeability that will only drive people to take you down. I'm not talking about walking through the halls of your company as if you own the place (unless of course you do). It's not being a bitch for being a bitch's sake. It's not instigating rudeness or gossip or looking to annoy people. What I am saying is that while our instinct is to be liked, true success demands respect—and respect simply doesn't come to the yes-girl whose coworkers walk all over her.

Here's an example. In one of my very first jobs, I was so excited to be working in a field that I loved, when a known bitch-of-a-colleague came into my office and said outright: I'm sick of you being the ray of sunshine around here. I had to make the choice. Nice girl (apologize for making her uncomfortable and take it down a notch) or mean girl (let her know I didn't really care what she was sick of and escort her out of the office).

Nice Girl = Liked

Mean Girl = Respected

More often than not, "mean" is a defensive position, rather than an offensive position. I didn't go out of my way to kick her out of my office, but in the face of a takedown I needed to make it clear I wasn't going to walk away the loser. I promise you, it doesn't matter what level you hit in your career, there are going to be instances when you will be pushed, and what the boss, assistant, client, boyfriend is looking for is feistiness. They want to know: Are you going to fight back or are you going to lie down? Lie down and you will be walked all over. And that brings us to the question: Is there a difference in being mean to my boss and being mean to my assistant? I'm an equal opportunity Meanie.

While being liked and respected aren't mutually exclusive, they are different. Like is a very subjective and generally fleeting feeling. It's defined as something we take pleasure in. This season it's plaid; next season it's metallic. Respect, on the other hand, is more objective. It's quantifiable and can be measured. It's based less upon opinion and more on performance. And performance is where your focus needs to be.

Here's the danger. The nice girl focused on being liked is in a never-ending, losing battle. Not only are the masses fickle—they are generally lazy and threatened by the mean girl's willingness to step up and demand attention and results. The mean girl is focused on surrounding herself with people who inspire and challenge her—not in building a fan club.

Let's put it this way: Anna Wintour isn't winning any boss of the year awards, but I don't know that she's losing any sleep over it in her West Village townhouse. And here we come to the other part of the equation: Anna is flocked on both sides with people clamoring to work both with and for her. Why?

Because the mean girl is always in demand.

Keep Him Keen

You're going to need to trust me on this one, but I want you to do a little experiment to prove something to yourself. You know the person who doesn't delight in you and your ideas the way you're generally accustomed? You know how you try extra hard to make her like you? I want you to turn it around. You play the bitch. It works like a reverse magnet. As Sherry Argov so brilliantly puts it in *Why Men Love Bitches,* "The person who is least dependent on the outcome of the relationship will automatically draw the other person in." The meaner you get, the nicer she'll become.

The mean girl captures the attention, demands the respect, and sustains the interest of everyone around her—she keeps them keen.

It's Not Personal . . . It's Business

What's the number one sign that we're too concerned with being the nice girl? We take it all too personally. This is a tough one because in one breath I'll tell you your career is all about you—your passion, your responsibility, your investment—but in another I'm adamant that there is a critical point at which you need to get over yourself in order to ask for what you want, take a risk, and know that this isn't a popularity contest. Mean girls understand it's not personal, it's business.

Mean girls aren't afraid to be told no

This isn't a scientific study, but time and time again, I do the same experiment in my business and in mixed-gender seminars and find the same result. Here's the scenario:

> a. *Guy asks for a raise. I say no. He thinks I'm an ass.*
> b. *Girl asks for a raise. I say no. She thinks* she's *an ass.*

The number one reason why we don't get what we want in our careers is we don't ask for it. And the reason we don't ask for what we want? We allow "no" to feel too personal. But you can't escape no—it's a part of the success landscape. So get over it. And then devote your energy or anger into figuring out what they *will* say yes to.

Mean girls protect their egos

Guys are experts at protecting their egos in order to risk rejection: "It's her loss. It's a numbers game. They don't know what they're missing." If you allow yourself to feel personally vulnerable each and every time you put yourself out there, you won't take the risks you need to in order to succeed.

Here's an admittedly cheesy trick that's helped me to keep some distance between my personal and professional persona. I grew up being called Nikki. My father, with visions of his daughter turning into a stripper, convinced my mom that the more professional "Nicole" on my birth certificate would be to my advantage. He was right. I will always be Nikki to my friends and family, but for professional purposes I step into Nicole. Don't take my word for it. Beyoncé Knowles has an alter ego she calls Sasha Fierce. She steps into that persona as she goes out on stage, and on some level it not only empowers, but protects her. Get yourself a nickname.

Mean girls don't work to be liked, they expect it

You gotta love the boys. I recently had a conversation about respect with a male colleague and he said, without hesitation, "Respect you need to work for, but I expect to be liked." I love this sentiment. If you go in with the *expectation,* rather than the *desire,* you're way ahead of the game. People who so desperately want to be liked rarely are. It's the want to be liked that keeps you ordering the birthday cakes and focused on the gossip rather than what really counts: your career. If you expect people to like you, they will.

Mean girls are good to their own

I'm asked this question frequently enough to warrant bringing it up here. Yes, I think that women can be a special kind of nasty to each other and it's a problem firmly planted in the personal. When we take things too personally, we look at another woman's success and begrudge it rather than admire it, we hear criticism as a personal affront, and we compare with an eye of resentment. As a boss, I promise criticism is a compliment. I don't know too many people who enjoy telling someone they suck. So when it happens that you're given direction, don't cry, don't scream, don't hold a grudge, don't get defensive—ask yourself if she's right and say thanks. If she's taking the time to criticize, consider that she may be telling you these things because she wants to help make you better. That cultivating your talent is actually worth her time and effort.

Mean girls use jealousy to their advantage

Mean girls not only understand that the world of work is not a place to live out our insecurities by taking each other down, but are confident enough in their own ability that they extend themselves and support their own. They also welcome competition because it forces them to up their ante and outperform the neophyte just waiting to take their place. While no one likes being jealous of someone else, envy happens. The key is to use those feelings to force yourself to do the hard things you've been putting off. Have the pity party and then figure out how you're going to get whatever it is you want. If she can do it, so can you.

The Tough Talk

While I've known plenty of women who won't hesitate to pick a fight with their guy, the majority of us try to duck out of hard conversations at the office. Though the "mean" conversation may look like an art, it's actually a science. Here are the five things you need to know about talking tough.

Get the facts

Before you make an ass of yourself, it behooves you to do some discreet research. What *exactly* did she say about you behind your back? Did he take *all* of the credit? Are you *really* paid 30 percent less than your colleagues? Get the down and dirty before you go face to face and make a fool of yourself without having the facts.

Catch them off-guard

Logic would suggest you want to ask for a designated time to actually sit down and have "the talk," but in the majority of cases a confrontational tête-à-tête is actually better had on the fly. Catch them in the hall, walking out of the building for the day, or stop by their office unannounced. You'll find your offender a little off balance and will get a more authentic response. This keeps the power ball in your court.

Ask the question

Again, with the goal of maintaining the balance of power, instead of launching into an "I-heard-that-you" tirade, ask the question: Did you . . . call me a bitch, steal my idea, sabotage my PowerPoint, read my BlackBerry? Not only does a question put them on the defensive, they often hang themselves and offer more incriminating evidence. In all honesty, a lot of would-be altercations are diffused at this point. Many a confrontation is built up to tizzy proportions based upon false accusations and misinformation.

Q & A

If I've said it once, I've said it a thousand times. I have a guy on my team who simply doesn't listen to me and continues to send in substandard work. How do I deal with this guy?

Sometimes "mean" is better demonstrated with action, rather than words. Simply give the assignment to someone else. Nagging him to make it better leads him to believe that he's indispensable and that he's the one with the power to fix it . . . or not. The moment you take it out of his hands, he'll feel threatened and very quickly buck up. If not, you've got someone ready and willing to take his place. You might want to try this one at home.

Keep the tears at bay

If you're dealing with a particularly emotional issue—talk, cry, or scream it out with friends who are not at all connected to work. You want to have your thoughts, your points, but most especially your emotions in check. I have seen people lose most of their credibility and all of their leverage in the face of the ugly cry.

Stick to the program

This is a hard conversation—hard as in firm, solid, and based upon fact. As I said earlier, start with the question, and if your findings are confirmed, be prepared with what specifically you want out of the conversation. Do you want him to make a public apology, go back to your boss and acknowledge it was your idea, or set up a scheduled discussion to determine what you need to accomplish in exchange for a promotion? This is one conversation you want to come away from with a clear deliverable so he knows you mean business . . . and good God, so you don't need to have it again.

Trick of the Trade: Make Them Wait

If someone got to this book first and uses my rules of confrontation, here's the secret antidote . . .

The biggest mistake people make in being confronted is to react immediately. You have every right to, and quite frankly should, hold your tongue. Feel free to use the question-ask strategy. "Where did you get that information?" is always helpful. After encouraging the other person to state his case, ask for a few moments, hours, days (depending upon the magnitude and what you can get away with) to think about it and get back to him.

Chapter 3

Leave Your Dad Out of It

I've heard it with my very own ears. Big meeting. Big boardroom. Big guns. When a young woman is asked to give her opinion, she begins with, *"Well, my dad thinks . . ."* That's when I, and everyone else in the room, turn off. Rest assured, no one cares what your parents think, and here's a hint for you: If dad gives you a doozy, claim it as your own.

In all honesty I thought I was going to have trouble finding inspiration and digging into this rule (which is really a call to grow up), but after working on a project for the past week with a twenty-one-year-old eager beaver, I've come to believe this chapter is more important than ever. Both in terms of helping you youngsters project some maturity and giving us (slightly) older girls a little lesson in how to work with you without wanting to slit our (and your) wrists.

Lies Parents Tell Us

Here's me breaking my own rule: My dad can be a bit of an ass. While most fathers were providing their kids a healthy dose of unconditional love, mine would make me earn it. And while his tough love approach may not have been good for my ego, in hindsight it's been great for my career. I meet a lot of younguns who still believe the (well-intentioned) lies their parents tell them, and I promise that it's believing you really are the center of the universe that's going to keep you out of the corner office more than anything else. Below, I've taken the classic lies our parents tell us and—channeling my dad—give you the real world truth.

You can do anything

Don't be delusional. If you could do anything, you'd be painting the *Mona Lisa* and dating Johnny Depp. Some things—like singing—take talent that only God can give you. You've seen those tone deaf teens on the *American Idol* audition tapes. Clearly their parents thought public humiliation was better than the truth.

You're special

No . . . you're not. There are about 10,000 other yous in a fifteen-mile radius who can do everything you can do, and half of them will work for less than you're currently making [and half of those would be happy to forgo the 401(k) match]. If your company outsources, multiply that number by 100. Never consider yourself irreplaceable—remember that after you've downed a few martinis and get the urge to tell your boss she's nothing without you.

Just be yourself

Are you kidding?! Do you really want everyone at the office to know you're an overly sensitive, insecure, not-as-smart-as-you-pretend-to-be borderline personality case? Instead, act like a hard worker. Find the person in the office whom everyone looks up to (just one level above you—don't think you can start acting like the CEO) and emulate her. Maybe someone will think you are the new whatever-her-name-is.

If you had fun, you won

Hey, if you had fun and still have your job (or at least didn't end up in the HR Department begging forgiveness), you won. But to really win, you have to *not* have fun. In fact, you'll probably have to suffer. Sure, suffering has its fun elements (hard work is fun in its perverse kinda way). But there is a reason they pay you to do your job— because no one will do it for free. Because it's hard. Because it can be tedious. And no one gives you points just for showing up. There are no participation trophies in the real world.

You did a good job

You did an okay, substandard job. If you're lucky, your work is half as good as your boss could do in a quarter of the time, hung over with a raging migraine. If you're lucky, your maximum effort is just enough to prevent your boss from throwing you overboard, so don't let up.

Sharing is caring

Keep everything for yourself.

A little hot cocoa makes everything better

Okay, that one's true.

Why It's Good to Be . . . and Hire . . . Young

I'm a bona fide cougar (love to date the younger boy) so I come to this discussion of the merits of youth with both experience and confidence. I've taken what I hear out of the mouth of babes and broken it down into (a) *why's it good to be young* if you're reading this and are under twenty-one (or still act like it), and (b) *why it's good to hire young* for the rest of us who are stuck working with a tike.

"I can do anything."

Why it's good to be young: The best thing about youth is that life hasn't kicked you in the ass yet. As a youngun you haven't had your heart broken by the boss who steals your idea, or been disappointed by the fact that you're still working in a cubicle three years later. You still believe that you can be anything and that it's everyone's sole job to get you there. Remember this time . . . it's fleeting.

Why it's good to hire young: While this eternal, "I can do anything" optimism can feel trite and, frankly, exhausting as an employer, the key is to harness it all the way to the dreaded-task bank. At this stage, for example, your young protégée thinks that business travel is out of this world. It feels glamorous and she gets to tell her friends she's going to—wait for it—Portland. Don't feel guilty about giving her what feels like the dirty work—she's having a blast.

"I'll try anything."

Why it's good to be young: Kinda like gymnastics, when I got back into the world of dating, there was a whole new level of acrobatic ability that somewhere along the line had become the norm. You not only know what's cutting edge, but have an ability to look at old ways of doing things and give them an exciting twist.

Why it's good to hire young: You would have wasted fifteen minutes on the phone bribing the receptionist for a CEO's e-mail. Your new hire looks him up on Facebook and has an "in" in seconds. They've got new words, networking tools, and news outlets that haven't yet trickled up to your age bracket. Use it to your advantage and put them on a project you've been frustratingly stuck on. They may surprise you with a new idea, perspective, or position.

"But why?"

Why it's good to be young: Love the curiosity and the admission that you don't know it all, but sometimes it's enough to know you're photocopying that pile of paper because I told you so.

Why it's good to hire young: I learned the trick to this one. The more you share the whole picture—explain the impact her contribution is going to make on the entire project, company, universe—the more motivated she becomes. It's an investment to share the details, but I promise not only will her deliverable be superior, she'll feel appreciated—which pays off big in the end.

"Sign me up."

Why it's good to be young: It's hard to believe at twenty-one, but this level of energy and endurance doesn't last forever. In all likelihood, *you* are your only responsibility and that means you should be raising your hand for weekend assignments and after-hours events. Pay your dues now before you're too tired and committed to want to do the late-night scene.

Why it's good to hire young: The young buck has insatiable energy, trying everything in his power to pleasure you. Take advantage of it.

"Here, let me drive."

Why it's good to be young: You were born with a mouse in your hand, and your single biggest asset is that you've got this whole technology thing down pat.

Why it's good to hire young: Let them lead the way. This is one area of your business, regardless of how irritatingly right they are and how quickly things change, where you have to be willing to hand over the reins. They'll ride you into digital victory.

Act Your Age

Here's a horrifyingly true story: I'm in NYC's Penn Station with one of my team when the conductor on our train to Boston asks her if she has her mom's (that'd be me) ticket. That would be possible if I conceived her at a premenstrual six. Now I can go in one of two directions with this one: Do I look too old or does she look too young? It's my book so I'm going to blame this one on her (and maybe him considering his Rudolph red alcoholic nose and the fact he reeked of liquor—obviously a blurry-eyed drunk). I've got a whole chapter coming up on your looks, but let's just say that if you want to be taken seriously, tightless miniskirts, belly-baring T-shirts, and Chuck Taylors are no-no's in the work wardrobe. And if you're over twenty-one, I'd strongly suggest you remove those items from your "on the town" arsenal as well.

Which brings me to my next point: It's not only how you dress that makes you look young, it's what comes out of your mouth. The same can be said for how you communicate over e-mail. Leave the LOLs, BRBs, and TTYLs for casual chats with your friends—not your colleagues. Remember you're cultivating a persona, an image, and unless you want it to scream sorority sister at the frat kegger, you've got to lose the college look and attitude.

Here they are, some clear signs you need to act your age.

This one time at band camp

Again, we get that your last major life stage and frame of reference is college, but honestly, it makes us feel old. Keep the pub-crawl-pulling-all-nighter-football-stand-mushroom-brownie conversation to a minimum.

Only room for one of us

I gave this one some thought and it comes down to the fact that at least here, at the office, as your boss . . . I need to be the most important. Your dad calling to let me know he didn't agree with your six-month review or the fact that your mom would like to meet me before you accept the job just tells me you're not ready for a new boss in your life—and there's only room for one of us.

Wipe your nose

We appreciate the vote of confidence, but we know we're not always right, or look great today, or dropped a couple of pounds, or are the smartest person you know. Stop kissing our ass.

Big girls don't cry

Nothing makes you look more delicate, vulnerable, and weak than crying like a girl. If you pull the tears card one too many times, we're not going to ask you to do the hard (career-enhancing) thing or have the hard (career-enhancing) conversation. Your loss.

Talent night

I'm mortified to think back and know I did this . . . repeatedly. I would invite people into my office for a reading. I liked writing and the pleasure was intensified by reading to others. Because I was looking at the page, I didn't notice my audience was nodding off. Show off your gifts, but this isn't talent night in your parents' living room.

How to Use Family Connections

So let's go back to the opening example. When your dad is Jack Welch, maybe they don't turn off. If you have parents with connections, don't be afraid to use them, but there are some rules involved:

1. Don't pull rank

It's kinda like sleeping with the boss and expecting that you're going to get ahead with ease. Not only do you need to overperform in order to prove you're not getting preferential treatment, but if you want to keep the resentment to a minimum, don't pull the trump card (even though we all know you can).

2. Make a name for yourself

Speaking of "trump," would Ivanka be the VP of Real Estate Development and Acquisitions at the Trump Organization without her family name? Based upon the interviews I've read . . . maybe. Your name will take you only so far. If you have any interest in actually earning respect, get ready to prove you're your own woman.

Trick of the Trade: Family Legacy

So not only is your family name not Hearst, you actually grew up with Mommy Dearest. Some of the most successful people in the world came from nothing and, even worse, total and utter dysfunction. The same way your ass of a father (mother, brother, uncle) impacts all of your personal relationships, he's going to affect your career as well. And the same way you have a choice to use the power of experience for good (to motivate you) or for bad (feel sorry for yourself) in the bedroom, you have the same decision to make in the boardroom.

3. Trust your gut

Being loved for your name and what it has to offer him is a pretty sad and lonely existence. You need to be extra careful to steer clear of the moochers.

Chapter 4

Keep Your Mouth Shut

J ust like you want to refrain from raising the freak flag on a first, tenth, fiftieth date, there really are some things that no one, not the least of which your boss, needs to know about you.

Too Much Information (TMI) is running rampant in the world of work, and one of the most strategic things you can do to set yourself apart is to keep your mouth shut. In a world of open work space and Facebook, discretion has become an art you need to master.

I get that long hours and intense environments are fodder for friendships, but what you need to remind yourself is that these are your coworkers. Unlike a friendship born out of choice, day after day you need to be prepared to face these people who now know that your favorite position is doggie style. There is a necessary distance that's required in order to maintain not only a level of efficiency, but also an air of mystery, and in a lot of cases . . . respect.

Things Better Left Unsaid

The thing about TMI in the office is that the lines are blurry. We spend more time with our colleagues than we do with our best friends, yet we don't have quite the same perspective, understanding, and appreciation—which makes it's hard to retract those "I hooked up with a married guy" tidbits about ourselves we'll regret sharing as soon as they're past our lips. Because it can be hard to determine how far is too far in the office setting, I've pulled some examples to make this whole TMI thing crystal clear. If you begin to utter these words, bite your tongue.

- **"I'm going to take a pregnancy test at lunch . . ."**

It's just a general rule of thumb to stay away from any conversation that has to do with your private parts—the tantric sex you had last night, the abortion you're considering, the raging yeast infection—all stuff that really shouldn't be shared. They're called your privates for a reason.

- **"Don't tell anyone, but . . ."**

Remember that game of telephone we played in grade school? Not only can you count on your secret not being kept, but expect it to take on a life of its own. By the time your little secret crush on the FedEx guy makes the rounds, you'll have blown him in the boardroom.

- **"You're a bitch . . ."**

"Nikki put a hickey on Ricky's dicky." I was five when Scott Duncan pulled this one out of his hat. I didn't know what a "hickey" or a "dicky" was, but it stuck with me. There are some things that, once said, cannot and—will not ever—be forgotten. In the face of a knock-'em-down fight with a coworker, steer clear of the name-call.

- **"My mother is manic-depressive . . ."**

You'd like to think your family issues don't reflect on you, but they do. Just like a guy is checking out your mom to see just how fat you're going to be in twenty years, your colleagues are wondering if you're going to slit your wrists now that you've lost a major client.

- **"God made me to do it . . ."**

Chalk it up to intuition, past experience, insider scoop. Unless you're working in a convent, religious beliefs don't belong at the office.

- **"I put myself through college by stripping . . ."**

The unsavory parts of your past should absolutely be kept under wraps—and off your Facebook page. When you're giving a presentation to the staff, do you really want them to imagine you pole dancing?

- **"I think my boyfriend's cheating on me . . ."**

I've never understood why girls give that up on a date, not to mention at the staff meeting. It's kinda like saying: "Hey, he doesn't think I'm worth it . . . neither should you."

- **"I hate my job . . ."**

That may very well be true, but this isn't the time or place.

Trick of the Trade: A Virtual Unknown

You'd think I wouldn't need to mention this, but based on the fact that I just took a quick stroll online and found the bare breasts of a woman we're considering hiring, apparently I do. Just like you wouldn't consider going out with a guy without Googling him, your employers, clients, coworkers—they're all vying to learn a little more about you and are doing the same. If you've got a Facebook or MySpace page, set it to private and refrain from putting pictures on it that you wouldn't want a potential employer—or your mother—to see. MySpace doesn't actually mean "my" space. If you're looking to reveal the inner you, go old school and get yourself a journal and hide it under your mattress.

Don't Talk

Please make it stop. I'm rolling into the second hour of a monologue that seriously demonstrates not only how wildly incompetent the woman talking is, but how sickeningly narcissistic she is to boot. There's not a thing about my stifled yawns, BlackBerry check, or glossy eyes that are signaling I'm bored to tears. I would have excused myself about fifty-five minutes ago but I'm doing a favor for a friend who will now owe me her firstborn. When we're nervous . . . we talk. When we feel unprepared . . . we talk. When we're underqualified . . . we talk.

Note to self . . . don't talk.

Every certified business genius I've met has something in common—they're able to choose their words carefully and wait for the golden moment to seal the deal. We think in order to impress, the name of the game is to say anything that will stick. But conversations, whether in dealing or dating, are about quality, not quantity. To know what to say and when, you've got to know what's relevant. And you won't have a clue about what that is unless you stop talking.

But enough about me

The trick to refraining from talking ad nauseam about yourself? Ask a question. Questions are the most powerful relationship-building tool you have in your career arsenal. If used correctly, they are the means of controlling conversation, the flow of information, and the creation of intimacy. You'd think question asking would be easy, but it's really an art form:

- **One at a time.**

I have a major issue with the double ask. Looks something like this: "What's your favorite movie?" and before the person can answer . . . "Did you see *Breakfast at Tiffany's*?" Ask a single question and don't freak at the silence. Give him a fighting chance to produce an answer.

- **Don't be a know it all.**

While sometimes you need to employ this directional tactic, "You don't really think we should use that font" is *not* a question—it's a statement.

- **It's not a deposition.**

Fire one too many and the conversation turns into an interrogation. There is a law and an order to asking questions. The law: Slow and steady wins the race. The order: Take turns.

- **Think before you ask.**

Voltaire had some killer insight. "Judge a man by his questions, not by his answers." "How many sick days am I entitled to?" says as much about you as the answer reveals about them.

- **Practice enlightenment.**

Consider yourself a master if your partner-in-conversation walks away feeling as if he just had an amazing therapy session without having to pay for it. Helping others to see a situation in a new light is priceless. Keep "Have you ever considered . . ." or "Where do you imagine . . ." up your sleeve.

- **Get them to spill it.**

The quickest way to have people feel as if they know *you*? Encourage them to spill. Intimacy is a funny thing. We feel closest *not* to those we know the most about, but those who know the most about us.

- **Listen up.**

What was said: "I don't ever want to get married." What you heard: "Maybe someday . . . soon." There's no point in asking a question if you're not willing or able to actually hear the answer.

Life of the Party

Nothing makes people avoid you like the plague like not being able to keep a conversation flowing. Just as important as knowing *how* to ask questions is knowing *which* questions to ask so that you aren't left with awkward silences. Keep these essentials on hand at all times and watch as you propel from "Where'd everyone go?" to "In the know," without having revealed too much!

The open-ender: "Where are you from?" "How did you become interested in this industry?"

You've got nothing but time on your hands (the next train is an hour away) and you're too tired (or drunk) to talk. This is the perfect opportunity for an open-ender—a chance to let your conversation partner go where he wants to go—which is invariably exactly where you need to be. When you're just getting to know someone, where he ends up going is very telling. Not only will it give you a point to reference, but it will provide you with some Google-able tidbits to follow up on.

The relevant: "I read you went to Cornell. What was it like going to school there?"

You've already implemented your sneaky Facebook-stalking tactics to find out a thing or two about him. Now you're ready to flatter him with a personalized and thoughtful question. Careful here, though. Make it too relevant and you can find yourself with your foot in your mouth. Make sure your source is reliable, updated, and public enough that he won't think you're creepy.

The clarifier: "I'm not really sure what you mean when you say . . . can we go over that again?"

We're all great at selectively listening, but when we only hear what we want, we run the risk of misinterpreting. A clarifier allows you to clear up confusion and gives you a minute to catch up when your brain is running on empty. It's also perfect for when you've just heard someone speak and you want to buy some extra time with the expert.

The redirect: "We can talk about that another time. But for now I'd really like to hear more about . . ."

The redirect worked like a charm for me recently when a high-ranking producer asked for my opinion on her TV show's ad. A quick "What do you think?" revealed that she hated it, and would have hated *me* if I hadn't agreed. This type of question is great when you're unsure how to answer, or you don't want to reveal too much. But overuse it and you run the risk of looking like an idiot.

The reiterater: "So you'd like to . . ." "So you prefer . . ."

Unlike the clarifying where you're after more info, this is simply a repeat—it's like saying, "Are you sure you don't want to change your mind on that one?" It also lets you cover your ass—if he meant what he said, he can't call you out when you hold him to it.

The hypothetical: "What would you do in a situation where . . . ?"

Does this person have a thought of his own? Does he have the ability to empathize? Is he the glass-half-full type? The hypothetical will tell you all you need to know about his attitude.

The confidence builder: "You're a talented ____. Where did you learn that?"

What's crucial here is the statement that prefaces the question. A little ego boost will soften someone up like butter, ready to spill his secrets.

The elaborator: "Tell me more about . . ."

Now we're talking second date material. You've already got the basics down and you want to dig a little deeper. The elaborator is a great way to keep him talking and it gives him permission to open up to a new level of intimacy.

The feeler: "How do you feel about . . ."

It's called a feeler for a reason—it's emotional, it's raw, and it can be quite heated. Though this can be the most effective type of question for getting the information you need, it also has the most piss-off potential. "How do you feel about kids?" "What's your opinion on the situation in Israel?" If you're going to go there, be ready for the answer. And make sure they're ready to be asked.

The most important question there is: "How can I help?"

The body never lies

As I've well learned, when you're busy yapping, you miss out on a valuable opportunity to read between the lines. In one of my first publishing meetings, I encountered an editor who grilled me in a way that indicated all bets were off. I said to my agent on the way out, "Well, that was a bust," and she said, "No way. Didn't you see his pupils?" As it turns out, body language can be way more indicative of what a person actually thinks than what comes out of their mouth. There are some subconscious and physiological symptoms of attraction—whether in the context of a bar or a boardroom—that reveal you're turning him (or yes, her) on:

His pupils will dilate. Pupils enlarge for two reasons—to adjust to the light or because they're intrigued. So if you can't see the color of his eyes past his pupils and the room ain't dark, keep working at it.

He'll scan your entire face with his eyes. Have you ever been in a conversation with someone and you notice they're staring at your lips or your ears? It's no coincidence that these are your erogenous zones, and he's trying to take in as much as he can. Let him eat his heart out.

The trunk of his body will face you square on. It's like when you ask a guy if he's ready to get married and he shifts his entire body to the side and says "Sure." You'll know he's seriously considering commitment when his eyes *and* his body are centered on you.

He'll cross his leg toward you. If he's sitting next to you rather than across the table, look for his foot pointed in your direction. Feet, like the ears and the lips, have a concentration of nerve endings—and he's inching as close as he can into your personal space.

He'll jump at any opportunity to touch you. He asks if he can take your coat and grazes your arm when he reaches for it. He guides you into the room with his hand on the small of your back. You make a joke and he grabs your shoulder as he laughs. I've used touch before and it backfired when the VP followed me to the bathroom asking for some more . . . use your own discretion when reciprocating on this one.

His eyes will water. He may blame his allergies or say he's got a sneeze coming on, but his glossy eyes are nature's way of letting him get a clearer picture of you.

He'll stroke his tie or lapel. A subconscious enactment of what he'd like to do later, but still a good sign.

He'll tilt his head. It's the same thing my dog Missy does when she's begging for my affection—it's animal instinct that can't be denied. Now that you know you've got his attention, keep delving into the topic at hand.

If he's not giving anything away and you're still confused about how he feels, there are three more surefire signals you can watch for. When these are revealed, though, heads up—the hook-up potential is not in your favor.

Slow nodding. Although nodding is known to signify an agreement, the secret is in the pace. While a slow nod signifies a person understands, a speedy one shows they're growing impatient. And if they're nodding yes while uttering the word "no," beware—motioning the opposite of what's being said is a sign of hidden motives. Who knew a nod could be so complicated?

Tapping toes. If the guy can't stop tapping his toes, drumming his pencil, or doing any other action repeatedly, he's either fiending for another hit or he's got more important places to be. Up his intrigue with more substantial subjects until his hands stop shaking, or move on to someone who feels you're worth his time.

No eye contact. If he's looking down at the table while he's talking to you, or faces his friend every time he responds to a question, there's a good chance your cohort's claims are riddled with white lies. However, if his eyes are scouring the room as if he's counting all the exit signs, he's just plain bored to tears. Pull out some juicier details or be ready for them to announce "a family emergency."

The Last Word

Silence is golden. Try it.

Chapter 5

If You've Got It, Flaunt It

L et's start with the broad strokes. I just took a quick look at the latest stat, and men think about sex every 52 seconds; that's over 1,661 times a day. Now with 70 percent of that waking day spent at the office, to think that this isn't playing into your career is not only absurd, it's naïve.

Career success is based upon leverage. Leverage is defined as "positional advantage." You have a number of assets to position to your advantage—talent, humor, discipline, creativity, and yes, I'm going to say it: your sexuality.

There comes a point in all of our personal lives when we realize just how powerful we are as women. A coy smile and tilt to the head can be all it takes to get our own way. This power exists at the office as well, and if you've got it . . . flaunt it.

What Is "It"?

Actually, let's start with what "it" isn't. It's not a plunging neckline, it's not acting stupid, it's not Giselle-like looks and it's definitely not an exchange of sex for a promotion—that has a whole other name.

What I'm talking about is an intangible energy. It is a stand-up-straight kind of confidence. It is lightness and ease. It is a sense of humor that comes with not taking yourself too seriously. It's captivating and commands attention.

"It" is power.

Dirty Little Secret

I've had this conversation many times before and can hear the outrage now. I know many a woman who believes she is way above the use of her womanly wiles. I was doing a television interview not long ago with a dynamic and, frankly, very attractive woman. During our on-air conversation she pushed and pushed, and suggested I was personally responsible for setting the feminist movement back fifty years. At the end of the interview, cameras off, I had to say it: "Are you kidding me? You're telling me you have never used the fact that you're a beautiful woman to your career advantage?"

She replied quickly, "Of course I have."

Most people intellectually refuse to play the game, assuming it degrades and discredits them—but in actual fact, they're doing it, even if they aren't consciously thinking or talking about it. Let me be crystal clear. I believe in women with everything in me. But I'm also a realist. I think we've had way too many years of presuming that the key to success for women is to pretend that we're men.

The key to career success is using all the tools you have available. You are a woman. You have special qualities, not the least of which is your ability to possess charm and stimulate attraction. This isn't about having sex in order to get ahead; it's about acknowledging that there is power in desire and using that to your advantage.

Trick of the Trade: Note to Self . . .

Do you work with all women and think this chapter doesn't apply to you? Think again. Women are as receptive to "it" as men. Remember this isn't about sex but *desire,* and in the case of work, the desire is to be a little more like you.

How Do You Get "It"?

For good or for bad, "it" is not a magical concoction that you can whip up and apply to yourself. Just like in dating, if you're putting on a personality and attitude that aren't yours, they feel false and uncomfortable to you and to everyone around you. The key to getting more "it" is becoming comfortable in your skin. So how do we do that?

Know that it's all in your head

The most powerful and frankly sexiest asset you have possession of is your brain. Who isn't attracted to people who are smart, articulate, and able to hold their own? If you want to build your "it" factor, pick up a book, engage in intellectually stimulating conversations, hit a museum. Another thing to consider is that "it" is a game of strategy—being smart enough to know who and where to apply your efforts. We'll talk a little more about this in the next section, but more than anything, you need to have your head screwed on tight.

Have a laugh

Honestly, in the space of career, the person whom others actually want to spend time with wins. If you want to play "it" in the workplace, you're going to need to be able to put down your defenses and allow yourself to have some fun. I'm not underestimating the significance of sexual harassment in the workplace, but in my experience where we run into trouble is when we take ourselves or others too seriously. The world of work should be enjoyable. Banter and flirtation are an important part of building relationships. I'm not talking about the boss who grabs your ass, but if someone says you look great today, assume the best and smile.

Dress the part

If you face the same "What's the easiest, most comfortable thing I can get away with?" urge as you look into the closet each morning, you don't have "it." "It" is knowing you're a big girl and are going to have to play dress-up for the day not only to convey an image of power and success to others, but to actually *feel* confidence in and of yourself.

One of my favorite quotes is from Diane von Furstenberg. She says, "I design for the woman who loves being a woman." You're a woman. Love being a woman. Dress like a woman. But, and this is a big but, dressing like a woman does not translate to dressing like a whore. I've written a whole chapter on how to pull yourself together, but for the purposes of the discussion of "it" (and because I encounter way too many women jacked up in their booby-bearing blouse, miniskirt, and 6-inch stilettos) both at the bar but even more frightfully at the office, now's the time to lay out the One Sexy Thing Rule. As with anything that lives in that gray area between personal style (sexy) and public perception (too sexy) . . . less is more. Never, ever don more than one sexy thing at a time. Here are your options:

Cleavage: Let me promise that no one's listening to your stellar ideas when all they can hear is: "Look at these, look at these." Because your boobs are so close to your face, they can be infinitely distracting if positioned for viewing pleasure. And please know the boys are not the only ones who are sneaking a peek—women can see them, too, and aren't nearly as impressed. Wear your low-cut blouses and sweaters but stock up on underpinnings— camisoles, undershirts, tanks—all essential when you want to ride the line between provocative and pornographic.

Legs: Truly, legs are the safest and most powerful way to suggest sexy without going over the line. Unlike our asses, most women are okay with their calves and able to show them off without feeling too revealed. Notice I mention calves. The most flattering and appropriate length hovers somewhere between an inch and two inches above the knee. If you insist on donning your babydoll, pull on a pair of tights and skip the platforms.

Feet: Speaking of shoes, Carrie Bradshaw has it all right. Slipping on a beautiful and sexy pair of heels is like dipping yourself in power. Not only do they help make your legs look long and lean, they're a fun and easy way of playing with color and style. But know that not every pair of kicks does the trick. The sound of your bare foot slapping the rubber of your flip-flop? Irritating. The look of you pitched forward trying to balance precariously on heels that are out of your reach? Ridiculous. Those callused heals and chipped toe nails? Sexy is in the details.

Walk tall

The good news for those of us who don't look like Kate Moss is that "it" is not about model good looks. Think Hillary Swank or Maggie Gyllenhaal. These women exude "it" by carrying themselves with poise and confidence. So much of "it" has to do with the way you hold yourself: your posture, the firmness of your handshake, your ability to look people in the eye without staring them down. This is the stuff that is born from confidence, but can absolutely be bred.

Know what turns you on

This concept is not just applied to the people you work with but the industry you're in and the company you work for. The more engaged, excited, and committed you are to your work, the more attractive you become to those around you. On some level I think we're all looking to get away from the feeling that our career is a grind, and if you can be the one who is focused on bringing passion and excitement to the office, you'll be the belle of the ball.

How Do You Flaunt "It"?

As with all power, it has the potential to be misused: You've heard
what they say about playing with fire. Not for a second do I underestimate how potentially dangerous bringing out the "it" actually
is—it's why I think it's worth focusing a chapter on it. The wrong
person in the wrong circumstances can be career suicide. The most
adamant recommendation I have for you going into this section is
this: Less is more.

Leveraging "it" for the sake of your career is a game of fine lines.
What's appropriate in some circumstances and with some people is
off limits in and with others. Your goal is to keep your eyes and ears
open and become sensitive to reaction, comfort, and boundaries.
The rules of flaunting are actually very reminiscent of the ins and
outs of flirting.

Make your mark

No one should be untouched by your charm, but just like you
wouldn't hit on someone out of your league, keep your efforts within
limits. Dallying with your boss's boss and those directly reporting
to you is infinitely more dangerous.

Follow their lead

Boundaries are a tough one as they're heavily dependent upon the
individual.

I know I can give my investment partner a big, familiar hug but I
didn't take that liberty until he reached out to me first. Just like at

the bar, you're looking for signs of interest, and if you can at all help it, you don't want to be the one making the first move. It's a game of matching—eye contact, a level of familiarity, physical distance, and touch—let him show you what's comfortable and then feel free to step in.

Trick of the Trade: It All Comes Down to the Pretty

It's a secret strategy that every woman must know by heart and be prepared to use in any and all circumstances.

If you want to disarm a fellow female, compliment her, and not on her brains, her stellar track record, or her performance. Go straight for her appearance. It doesn't matter how brilliant or physically unattractive she is, I've seen it work on all shapes and sizes. We love to feel pretty and we take a personal kind of pride in the physical attributes we feel most confident about. The trick is finding "the one." If you complimented me on my full lips, I would immediately dismiss you. My eyes, and I'd think you were wonderfully perceptive and had exquisite taste.

Find something that you authentically feel is worth complimenting (shiny hair, shapely legs, fabulous bag) and you've unleashed the surefire way of gaining the favor of any and all women.

Underpromise

This is one area you definitely do not want to overpromise and under-deliver on. I have seen women suggest both verbally and nonverbally that they are willing to pay a price for career advancement—and then aren't ready to deliver. No one likes a tease.

Pick your moments

Again, a lot like flirting, you don't want to take the big risk in front of a crowd. There are a couple of reasons for this: (a) no one wants to crash and burn in front of others, (b) keeping it private ensures he's not put on the spot, which he may resent, and (c) it doesn't make those watching either embarrassed for you or pissed off at you.

Chapter 6

Don't Bash Your Ex

S
o if I haven't mentioned it yet, I'm a dater. Love it, actually.
While it's most women's worst nightmare (especially in
NYC), I happen to enjoy the thrill and adventure of sitting across the table from a new guy wondering if he's
the love of my life (I may also have some commitment issues, but
that's a whole other book). So anyway, the other day, I was dining
with what was seemingly one of the hottest, smartest, wittiest
guys I'd met in ages. We dove into politics, reveled in our family
dysfunction, and skirted around the conversation of our exes. But
then he gained momentum. Bitch this, bitch that. And there it
was . . . the C-word. Now, I can swear with the best of them. And
she may very well be a C*@$, but I'm not considering her as a date.
I'm considering him and he told me everything I need to know: he's
a jackass.

Deal breaker. I don't care if it's your ex-boss, ex-colleague, ex-husband, ex-client. Don't talk shit about your ex. It doesn't make him look bad . . . it makes you look bad.

Eyes and Ears

I put gossiping in the bashing category, and while I know (from experience) a "no-gossiping" policy isn't going to fly in real life, you really do need to be careful. For one, it does make you look bad (somewhere between malicious and I have nothing going on in my own life), and even more than that, it suggests that you can't keep a secret. There are so many wonderful little gems out there that are going to help you in getting ahead in your career. Michael's doing Beth in the bathroom, a merger's going down, John's got a drinking problem—there's a lot you can do with this kind of information, but you're not going to get any of it if you're the one doing all the talking. If you do have a piece of juicy low-down that you need to share, divulge it with someone you trust outside of the office, but please, please be wary of . . .

Elevators

I don't know what it is about elevators, but when we're all contained in a two-by-three box, what makes you think we can't hear your whispers . . . and that we don't know your boss is named Mark . . . and that we aren't interested in the fact that he's buying his mistress flowers with the company AMEX?

Restaurants

This one is about volume control. Glasses are clinking, plates are crashing, and you're yelling. If you want to share the goods, keep it down to a dull roar and don't select the bar your assistant repeatedly hits for drinks after work.

E-mail

Shouldn't have to mention this but have seen it enough times to warrant a call-out. It's one thing to gossip, but don't be stupid enough to put it in writing.

Public transit

You'd think this would be a long shot, but who knew Maria's mother rode the 6 train? Far and wide, there are eyes and ears hanging on every glorious word you utter.

Trick of the Trade: A Note on the Competition

Maybe you're a tad bit jealous because she totally pulls off skinny jeans and she's tight with all the boys. Maybe you're feeling threatened because she's got the work ethic of a mule and she never seems to miss a beat. Bad-mouthing in-house competition is never (unless it's cleverly disguised as a compliment and said straight to their face) a good idea, and nine times out of ten you'll achieve the exact opposite of what you intended by opening your mouth. "Oh come on, she's not *that* pretty, and besides, I heard she pulls the trigger after every meal" will only make you look ugly. And "Little Ms. Know-It-All doesn't know shit" will make you seem like the one who's out of touch. Whenever you're tempted to flout your frenemy, consider what it is about her that's making you feel inadequate and use it as a wake-up call to reassess your weaknesses. Be thankful for that healthy little kick in the butt that will make you step up your game and realize what you're really made of.

Tell Me About Her

It's the question you can't avoid. Why did you leave your last job? You'd think they'd like to hear that your ex-boss is an ass and your company's going down the tube but they don't—at least not from you. The world of work is so very, very small, and the last thing you want to do is burn bridges. Here a few read-between-the-lines responses:

• **It was an interesting experience.**

Everyone knows that describing someone as "interesting" is just a nice way of saying he was out-of-his-mind crazy. The key is to let them come to that conclusion on their own.

• **I learned a ton.**

About what I would never, ever, ever do as a boss. Yes, everything can be chalked up to a "learning experience."

- **We outgrew each other.**

People get it—even the best of relationships come to an end. But they don't need to know that you found him in bed with your best friend, or that he promoted your coworker because she's got a tighter ass than you do.

- **It wasn't meant to be.**

A diplomatic way of saying you'd rather stab yourself in the eye than work for that man.

Foot in Your Mouth

I'm a great reference giver. I know what I'm looking for when I ask for a referral and appreciate detail, so I tend to lay it on thick. I got a call from someone looking for the goods on a former employee who was frankly the stupidest person I've ever met in my entire life—seriously, stupid enough to put me on his reference list. I may have used the words "incompetent ass." Then came the call. I'd been caught red-handed by my ex-assistant. So what do you do when confronted with your indiscretion? Read below:

First, you had your say, let him have his. Seriously, I walked across my office to close my door, placed the receiver down, put the call to speaker (with the volume low . . . no one needs to hear his tirade), pressed mute so he couldn't hear me typing, and continued to work. Blah, blah, blah. You want to let him get it all, and I mean *all,* out. This can last anywhere from ten to sixty minutes (most people will peter out within the hour), but the key is to have him expend his energy. He's likely to go around in circles and you'll hear the same point fifty times, but again, let him go at it: Better you than your competitor. In my case, I had the benefit of the distance of the telephone. If you get confronted in person, ask to sit down somewhere private and keep your face as sympathetic as possible or at least expressionless—all it takes is a little smirk or smile to get yourself into another wave of tirade.

When he was finally limp from exertion, it took everything in me not to rile him up again with a "But you really are an incompetent ass," but unless you want to have another go-round, now's not the time to rub salt in his wound. I've practiced this time and time again. All people really want and need is to be heard, and in a case where they feel wronged (justifiably or not), it comes down to a simple apology. The mistake we tend to make here is to try and excuse, justify, tit-for-tat their shitty behavior, but at the end of the day, if you want this over and done with, stick to "I'm sorry."

Whether he accepts your apology or not, it's his decision, but at this point you're free to leave. I'm not a big let's-try-and-be-friends kinda girl after an irreparable rift (or breakup). You were talking trash about him for a reason. It's not like you're looking for a new best friend here. Walk away and let what you hope to be sleeping dogs lie.

It's All About You

The true lesson in keeping gossip to a minimum comes when you're on the receiving end of the bashing stick. So what do you do when your Best Office Friend Julie tells you what she's heard on the street . . . and it's all about you?

Tell the truth or fess up

As we've seen a hundred times over in the gossip magazines, there is generally a kernel of truth to the trash. What about what you've heard is actually fact and what's fiction? You manage each differently. If you really are having an affair, stole the stapler, are being paid more than any of your coworkers, think about how you want to respond now that the truth is out. Generally speaking, it's best not to deny it at this stage—you'll then become known as a slut, a thief, a greedy girl . . . *and* a liar.

Seal the leak

As for the rumor, or the part of it that isn't true—you've got to put a stop to it. Do your due diligence and get the details—who's saying what—and confront the source. Go back to what I've written about the hard-conversation-confrontation in Treat Him Mean, but in essence, the trick is to ask the question before accusing. "What have you been saying about me?" is quick and easy. Whether or not someone admits to talking out of turn, it's unlikely to happen again if he knows he's on your suspect list.

Do damage control

Ask Bill, Kobe, or even John Edwards—they'll tell you the best way to control the damage (and stifle the gossip hags) is to own up to the indiscretion and face the music as quickly as possible. Take a lesson from Martha, who had the chance to regain respect and maybe even maintain her bona fide soccer mom status, but blew it when she refused to fess up. Was the punishment too severe? Possibly, but when people sense that pride is getting in the way of an apology, they start to ignore evidence and disregard facts. They'd be happy just to hear one thing: I'm sorry. Even if you find the consequence unfair, or you could name a handful of others who've gotten away with the same thing, offer a contrite apology to those you've offended—or else expect it to show up in your stock price.

Don't Bash . . . You

This is an issue I see running rampant. At the end of the day, if you talk shit about others, you'll look bad; but talk shit about yourself and you'll look worse. Here's the thing: People believe what you tell them so when you're all "I'm so stupid" or "I'm so fat," they're going to take your word for it.

These are things I never want to hear you saying about yourself:

I'm Tired. I don't care if you burned the midnight oil having the best sex of your life, you're *not* tired. Tired is a weakness. Tired is a cop-out. Caffeinate, hydrate, take a walk around the block.

I'm Bored. Then find something to do. You let your boss know you're bored and she'll find something for you . . . and I promise you won't like it.

I'm Fat. Here's the thing: People who really are fat don't bother to point out the obvious. Saying "I'm fat" is a blatant request for someone, anyone, to call out, "No you're not." Now everyone not only knows you're vain, but has noticed that your hips are actually expanding, too.

I'm Stupid. You are if you call it out. Okay, so you can't multiply or don't know the capital of Canada, but keep it under wraps. Focus on what you do know and arm yourself with the tools (calculator and a map) you need to compensate for your stupidity.

Chapter 7

Don't Expect to Change Him

*T*hings will be different this time. He's learned his lesson. It won't happen again.

Leopards, assholes, mammoth organizations, crazy bosses—they don't change their spots. I know way too many women who have slaved away for years, climbing an insurmountable ladder or working with someone who treats them like crap, hoping that one day the boss will finally come to his senses and start to give them the credit they deserve. I promise you this: it's never gonna happen.

From the day I started my career, I've heard the same statistic. Women hold 14.8 percent of all Fortune 500 board seats and make only 75.5 cents to every dollar a man makes. Drives me to drink. Not because the numbers vary so slightly year in and year out, but because the focus feels all wrong. The only way an organization (read it . . . boss, man, industry) is going to change is if it hurts. And the only way to make it hurt is by passing them by. Focus on making yourself the most powerful, talented, successful woman you can be and walk your talented ass over to the best, most deserving company you can find . . . even if it's your own.

A successful career, like a successful relationship, is all about picking the right partner. Rather than focusing on how you can fix your crappy situation, I'm going to show you how to define your standards in the first place and become a stellar selector of the one who deserves you.

Whatcha Looking For?

I'm not entirely sure why, but I'd never date a guy who wears a bracelet. Not a particularly rational reason for not making the cut, but one of my nonnegotiables nevertheless. Whether it's stored somewhere in your brain or scribbled on a scrap of paper, I'm guessing you have a list of what you want in a man. Witty, charming, smart, Yankees fan—whatever floats your boat. But do you know what you're looking for in a company, in a boss, in a business partner, in your coworkers?

Give it some thought. And then write it down. I know it sounds kinda *Secret*-esque, but I promise it works. My list is going to be different from your list—you may like a guy in jewelry—so you have to do your own. But here are my top must-be's to get you started. What you may be surprised to find (I was) is that your list of must-be's in your boss isn't so far off from what you're looking for in your beau. He must be:

Loyal

You only need to be stabbed in the back, cheated on, taken advantage of once to realize just how important loyalty is. Not wanting to stoop to their level, I won't get into the details, but know that I was taken over the desk by a business partner who went behind my back and allowed something I was working on to be taken out of my hands. In an ideal world all your agreements (employment contracts, freelance agreements, business relationships) will have clear written contracts that specify what's-what and protect your interests. But in the real world and more often than not, you'll be relying on goodwill and a handshake. Unfortunately, loyalty is demonstrated through action. Trust your instincts and look for warning signs. But at the end of the day if someone betrays you, don't give him the chance to do it again. And if you find loyal subjects, reward them and keep them close.

Inspirational

I asked one of my best friends who was about to get married what it was about her guy that made her know he was the one. She said, "He makes me want to be better than I really believe I am." I had always thought that the real deal is to find someone who accepts you exactly as you are, but I've been with that guy on multiple occasions and in the end it gets a little tired. I'm learning this one as a boss. If you respond with, "great," "perfect," "thanks" on too many occasions, both incentive and quality go down. We all want to be better than we really believe we are. Look for bosses, employees, clients who up your game, who provide constructive criticism, who challenge you to be more.

Fun

This is a new one for me—a reminder to update your list regularly: The truth is even if you're in a career or in a relationship with someone you love, there's a day-to-day grind involved, and for that, you want to be with someone who makes things fun. My new thing is surrounding myself on both sides (above and below) with people I enjoy, people with a sense of humor, people who take their jobs, but not themselves, too seriously. Life's too short and your career's too long to be surrounded by kill-joys.

If you're still having trouble identifying what you want, I can help you pinpoint what you don't:

The Pessimist: I had the grave misfortune of working with the most glass-half-empty person I've ever met and warn you to steer clear. Between fixating on who's out to screw him (um, *nobody*) and constantly telling me all the reasons why an idea *wouldn't* work, it was kinda hard to get anything done. Who wants to be on the team with the guy who's already decided you're going to lose?

The Manic: One day she offers to lend you her Prada purse and the next she hits you with it. You can't make someone take their meds, and there are simply some psychological issues you're not equipped to deal with. It's tough to be productive when you need to sleep/work with one eye open.

The Addict: Booze, poker, strippers, nose candy—if you can name her poison, it's too close to the office. Be wary of people with addictive personalities. Their personal issues will lead them to make bad professional choices and you risk being taken down with them.

Where the Good Ones Are Hiding

Now that you've decided that you don't want to work for every Tom, Dick, and Harry, it's time to turn up the effort in tracking 'em down. You know the drill:

Friends and family

It may be a little embarrassing to admit you're on the market and ask for friends' help but even worse to be broke, unappreciated, and in a job you hate. Make sure friends and family know you're on the prowl and see what comes back. A qualified referral is worth its weight in gold.

Out and about

Sounds clichéd, but you never know when or where you're going to find the job of your dreams. Don't be narrow-minded in terms of both what might be the right fit (who knew shopping was actually a career) or where you're going to find it (anywhere but your apartment really). It's not going to happen for you with your butt planted in front of the couch or by moping around your regular haunts.

Online

Not only does a little online trolling allow you to peruse available options, if you hit a resource like vault.com, you can get the inside scoop on the day-to-day reality of slogging it out at a number of real-life, employee-reviewed companies. And while e-mail is a great way of corresponding and a phone call can be a helpful next step, whatever you do, don't accept an offer without a face-to-face meeting. We can all be fooled by digital distance and doctored presentations. No different from a first date, you have an amazing opportunity in an interview to identify the ass and cut your losses.

Just like you should stay clear of certain coworker types, the following boss behaviors in an interview should have you running for the elevators.

Me, me, me, blah, blah, blah.

Great that he's in the sharing mood, but if he doesn't come up for air talking about all he's accomplished, how the company couldn't survive without him, or how all of his female colleagues worship him—hit the road. Like a boyfriend who will never be comfortable with you sharing the spotlight, a boss who only talks about himself is a waste of your time. Find a two-way street without a dead end.

Excuse me, let me just grab this call . . . again.

All eyes and ears should be on you, glorious, captivating, brilliant *you*. A boss who shows up late, is taking calls and checking e-mails, or seems more interested in skimming the *Wall Street Journal* headlines than learning why you're the one for the job is never going to pay you the respect and attention you need to get ahead.

Get Matt on the phone, *now!*

A basic level of respect for human beings is probably the most essential boss-like characteristic. How's his tone with his assistant? As with the date who scolds a waitress at dinner, any questionable behavior is just a sneak preview of what's to come once he becomes comfortable enough to reveal his true colors.

It's actually pronounced "finn-ance."

Constructive criticism is one thing, but if he's too quick to point out your flaws and establish his superiority, that's one chip you don't want to waste your time hammering away.

So tell me about your breast, er, I mean your *best* asset.

There are a lot of things about you that should be the center of attention during an interview, but your chest is not one of them. Sure, you look slammin' in your suit and stilettos, but you want to be loved for your brains. He'll never recognize your intelligent contributions and star potential when he's thinking with the wrong head.

Make or Break

There are only so many hours in a day and prime career years to work with. You know what they say about the dead horse. If you're still unsure if you should stay or cut your losses, here's a real-world checklist of what's tolerable and what's not.

Tolerable	Intolerable
Asking you to stay late.	Asking you to babysit her bratty brood of kids.
Asking for your opinion on honeymoon hot spots (hey, at least he thinks you have good taste).	Asking for your opinion on threesomes (oh, the visuals!)
Taking a personal message from your boss's ex-husband.	Relaying that the ex should "go fuck himself" as per your boss.
Copying you on every single e-mail she sends. (Annoying for sure, but you never know when that paper trail might come in handy.)	Berating you in an e-mail she sends to the entire staff (though again, two words: paper trail).
Asking you to order her lunch.	Asking you to pay for her lunch out of your own pocket.
Losing his cool under pressure (it happens to the best of us).	Losing his cool under pressure and not acknowledging it.

Telling you to follow his lead in a meeting.	Telling you to sit there and look pretty in the meeting.
Having to reschedule your six-month evaluation—again.	Dropping the ball on your one-year evaluation, too.
Letting you know what she really thinks of your filing skills.	Calling you Karen—when your name is Kara.
Telling you your idea is brilliant—right before he takes the credit for it.	Stealing your idea—and then giving the task of implementing it to your colleague.
Making several rounds of edits to your proposal.	Making several rounds of edits to your e-mails.
Being just a wee bit vague when assigning you a task.	Yelling at you when the project doesn't come out exactly as she intended. Hello, you're not a mind reader.
Playing favorites with a coworker who's got twenty-five years with the company (at least he's loyal).	Rewarding her for work that you do just as well.

Chapter 8

Play Hard to Get

They say that anything worth having is worth fighting for, and in the case of your career, that something needs to be you. We're working with basic human instinct here. People want what they can't have, what feels scarce, and what others have already confirmed is of value. You've lived this phenomenon many times over:

- You dump him, he lands a hot chick . . . you want him back.
- You see it, you want it, you can't afford it . . . you pull out your credit card.
- You meet him, you love him, you call him for the hundredth time . . . he runs for the hills.

In the land of romance, we call it playing hard to get. In the fantasy of fashion, we want what's unattainable (both the body and the bag). In the world of career, it's all about supply and demand.

The Law

I'm not going to lie to you, I'm about as far away from an economist as you can imagine but I live and date in Manhattan, where guys who would never get laid in any other city in the world are somehow surrounded by supermodels. There is only one explanatoin for this: it's called the law of supply and demand. And for the purposes of our discussion we're going to focus on the curves.

The Supply Curve

Here's the concept of the supply curve. When supply goes down, the price goes up.

I've drawn a little picture for you on the next page and have related it to something we've all experienced. The less time, energy, effort (supply) you give to your guy, the more he seems to value or appreciate you (price). Not accepting a date for Saturday after Wednesday, the fifteen-minute timer by the phone—these are "The Rules" that are all about limiting your supply in order to increase your value. The bottom line: If you want to make yourself more desirable . . . make yourself scarce.

It sounds kinda illogical—isn't my boss going to notice I'm only coming in from ten to one? But in the case of your career, we're not talking about the number of hours clocked (although if you follow the steps that follow, that's exactly the position you'll find yourself in), it's about making yourself a scarce commodity—as in providing what everybody else isn't. I've been a boss for a lot of years now,

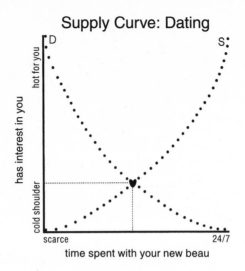

Be sure to deliver

It's not so much about the number of hours you spend sitting at your desk (or couch) but the experience you create and ultimately it comes down to this: Will you put out?

Believe me, getting someone to fill the chair isn't tough. There are literally thousands of people out there simply biding their time—coming into the office on Monday and counting down the hours (playing solitaire, checking out People.com) until Friday. Bosses and boyfriends alike are sometimes simply looking to fill the position—turning a blind eye to the fact that there's really nothing of substance being delivered. But I promise you another more interesting, attractive, captivating option *will* come along and you'll be left in the dust. Hard to value what's just sitting there looking pretty.

Let your work speak for itself

And you're not going to be able to deliver if all you're doing is talking. I'm all about tooting your own horn and taking credit where credit is due, but there's this fine line that, if you've experienced it, you'll know what I'm talking about. I've had this one-way conversation both personally and professionally and I'm not sure there's anything worse than some idiot telling you just how valuable, smart, or indispensable he is. If you're that great, word will be on the street and/or I'll come to that conclusion myself. You'd be surprised (or maybe not) at just how many lazy, entitled, unlikable people there are, who actually think (and won't hesitate to tell you) just how hot they are. The more time and energy you put into bragging about yourself, the less demand there will be for your talent.

Be a "special"-ist

There are plenty of pretty, nice, smart girls out there. What makes you so special? I have a simple rule. Don't even think about competing with the masses—you'll get lost in the crowd. I truly believe that if you want to set yourself apart, you need to figure out what you enjoy, which 99 percent of the time is what you're actually good at (why would you like if it you sucked) and then practice, practice, practice. Dedicate yourself to being the very best at your core talent—read everything you can get your hands on, take courses, attend industry events. I see way too many women who pussy-foot around, dabbling in this and then dabbling in that but never becoming an expert at anything. I know it's tough that you're good at a lot of things, but I promise you, bosses, vendors, clients—they pay for special talent—talent they can't find anywhere else. Pick a talent and be the best . . . better than all the rest.

Keep it fresh

Once you identify your special talent, you need to learn how to mix it up. Madonna has been dancing and singing for twenty-five years now, but we're still buying her next album, and if you're anything like my friends and me, you'll be first in line for tickets to her concert. Why? Because you always know you'll get something new. The key to working the supply curve is to deliver your core talent tied up in a sparkly new package. Regardless of industry, there's always innovation and you need to be ahead of the curve, changing your story, your appearance, your delivery so it feels unique (or in other words . . . scarce).

Not only is a healthy dose of reinvention good for others, it's good for you. I've been working on and pitching my business for almost eight years now, and there are seriously days when I bore myself to tears. Last year, in conjunction with a new business partner, and because I was tired of drinking my own Kool-Aid, we had a full-fledged reinvention—party and all. Same business—helping young women to build successful careers—but new packaging (website, name, brand colors), new team, and renewed energy. As I was writing my speech for the night, I came across the actual definition for "reinvention": *To make as if new, something already in existence.* I love this because it helps you to see that, really, it's not all that daunting. You don't—in fact, you shouldn't—have to start from scratch. Madonna really is the master of reinvention—each album, each video, each tour—still her, but somehow all new. Here are some specific ways you can do it yourself:

Make a change. You don't have to overhaul your personal brand or revamp your entire image every week, but small, subtle changes can keep you *and* others from getting bored with what you've got to offer. If your desk looks like it was plucked from the set of *The Office,* redecorate. If you've been handing out the same business cards since you applied for your DBA, design new ones. If you use Pilates class, a sick boyfriend, a root canal—*any* excuse to get out of happy hour with colleagues— surprise them and show up next time. Shaking things up will keep you engaged and others intrigued.

Learn a new trick. With competition constantly riding your ass, you've got to keep adding to your bag of goodies. Maybe taking a wine class will make you a more confident host at client dinners. Or perhaps experimenting with a different route to work will expose you to a new idea. No matter how trivial a new trick seems, keeping your eyes (and mind) open to a new way of doing things brings unforeseen opportunities.

Reevaluate. You can't stay current if you don't realize you're behind in the first place. Everyone needs a good reality check on a regular basis (some more often than others). Don't be the one who's clueless to her own obnoxious habits. Ask for input from others, identify your weaknesses, and then fix them.

The trick with the supply curve is that you really can get to a point of supplying less and getting more. If you build a unique talent, focus on delivering, and continually reinvent yourself, it becomes less and less about the hours you keep and more and more about the price you'll demand.

The Demand Curve

Here's the concept of the demand curve: The higher the demand, the higher the price.

Again, I've used an illustration and a relatable desire (fashion) to make the point.

Before we begin to explore the even more fun "demand" side of the play-hard-to-get equation, there are two things we need to consider.

First, I looked up the word "demand" and was struck by the definition: *"to ask for with proper authority."* A demand is not a demand without authority, and authority starts and ends with you. If

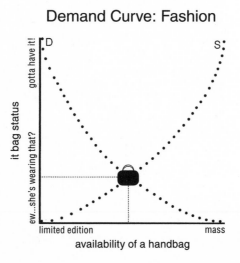

Demand Curve: Fashion

you don't believe you're worth it (love, money, respect), you won't get it.

Second, I'm all about barking up the right tree. In order to create demand, there needs to be an intrinsic desire. Don't get me wrong, desire is absolutely malleable—which is what I'll show you next, but let me put it this way: I've seen many a brunette trying to convince a blond lover she's the one (to love) and many a brilliant woman trying to convince a sexist boss she's the one (to promote). Both wasted a lot of time and energy. Choose your battles.

As for this battle, I've decided to use the Hermès Birkin handbag metaphor—not because you'd necessarily desire, let alone demand, one even if you did have an extra 5,000 to 50,000 bucks lying around—but it's an easy translation to your career. There are four key factors that affect demand: reputation, reliable quality, availability, and price.

Become known

As the story goes, while seated next to Hermès CEO Jean-Louis Dumas in 1984 on a Paris to London flight, British actress and model Jane Birkin opened her datebook and a flurry of loose notes fell to the floor. Conversation turned to the difficulty Jane had in finding the perfect leather weekend bag and voilà—weeks later it arrived on her doorstep—aptly named the Birkin. Let's be honest— there are lots of finely crafted options out there, but the Birkin is more than a handbag . . . it's a legend.

The goal is to become a legend. You need to be more than the hours you work and the product you deliver if you want to affect demand. You, your name, your reputation is the most powerful thing you have in creating demand. There are only twenty-four hours in each day, and in order to leverage your efforts and impact, you need to create a reputation that precedes you. How do you build a reputation? You repeatedly deliver something worth talking about.

Quality, not quantity

I picked up my first Birkin just recently, and as you'd imagine (considering the cost), it's a masterpiece. Hermès was originally known for making horse saddles for nobles. The quality was so outstanding that coronations would literally be held off waiting for delivery. Today, women are on waiting lists for weeks, months, even years for the privilege to pay big bucks for their very own Birkin.

If you want to increase your demand, you need to—not once, not twice, but *always*—deliver on quality. It doesn't matter how big or how small the project is, you need to commit your best effort, and even more than that, you need to exceed expectations. Pick your assignments carefully and less is more. I promise you'll always win if focused not on five half-assed projects but two stellar projects where you can produce significant results. If you're going to do a job, do it with everything you have in you. Just like we already talked about, figure out what your core talent is and do it on a level that no one can beat and you'll have employers, clients, and customers waiting in line to work with you.

Be unavailable

I wanted to see what would happen. I just called Hermès on Madison Avenue in Manhattan and let them know I'd be coming in an hour to buy a black Birkin. They told me no. I can't pick up a Birkin even with the money in hand because there are none available. How crazy is that?

I watch a respected friend and businesswoman do this all the time. She'll be asked to come in and work on a project and she says, "No." They call a week later, with 25k more in their budget, and she says, "No." The next week when they call with 50k more and she can do the consultation over the phone and doesn't have to fly to L.A. to implement her recommendations, she says, "Yes." I've asked her, "Don't you feel scared they'll just move on and hire another consultant (buy another bag)?" And she replies assuredly, "The harder I am to get, the more they want me—it doesn't decrease their interest, quite the opposite, it increases it."

Make them pay

The more it's worth (which is dictated by reputation and quality), the more people will pay. We're going to talk way more about this later on, but let it be known that the prohibitive price of the Birkin is a big part of its allure. It's a status symbol that says, "I'm successful enough to afford to carry this thing."

What you want to have happen in your career is to have companies fighting over the opportunity to pay you an enormous amount of money so they can say, "We're successful enough to attract this kind of talent." The more you ask for, the more they'll believe you're worth.

Chapter 9

Put on Some Gloss

*S*he's got a great personality . . .

We all know what that means and it isn't pretty. In a perfect world we'd all be respected, hired, loved, and promoted for our stellar smarts and winning personality but . . . we aren't. Instead, we have about 2.2 seconds to make a first impression and that straggly hair, booby-bearing blouse, and camel toe are speaking volumes.

I meet many a woman riding the moral high horse who insists she refuses to play the game. That it's her brains, not her bag, that matter, and I get it. But please don't be naïve enough to think for a second that people are not assessing you based upon your appearance. Your looks—and I'm talking everything from what you throw on each morning to how you style your hair—are communicating things about who you are and how you'll perform whether you like it or not. You can go in one of two directions with this little tidbit: Be angry and rebel by looking like shit every day or take control of the situation and pull yourself together. I recommend the latter.

Before we head into this chapter (and I'm stoned by feminists everywhere), let me start by pointing out three things:

- This isn't about model good looks. Your crooked nose, high forehead, and the extra ten pounds sitting on your ass—all just fine. In fact, if you're too physically striking, this can work against you in the world of work (we average-lookers can get a little jealous and take your beauty out on you in a myriad of underhanded ways). What we're really talking about is using what you've got and putting on a little gloss.

- I'm not suggesting for a second that you try and contort yourself into something you're not. Taking on a look that feels uncomfortable . . . looks uncomfortable. You can and should have your own style (but again, don't be silly enough to believe your tongue ring is going to fly in the majority of companies). For most of us, it's simply a matter of getting off our lazy ass, doing some shopping, and putting a little effort into the grab each and every morning.

- In the words of style icon Coco Chanel, "A girl should be two things: classy and fabulous." If you don't feel fabulous, it doesn't matter what you're wearing. At the end of the day, investing some time and energy into your looks—while helping others feel good about you—is really about making *you* feel good about *you*. To all my moral-high-ground friends, if you dig deep, I know you know that feeling of both pleasure and confidence that comes with a pretty polish.

A Dress for Every Occasion

For the most part, we've been practicing situation-appropriate dressing since time immemorial, but for some reason, a lot of us have difficulty making the leap from the personal to the professional. This'll help.

Out on the town = networking

So here's the deal: You think long and hard about the image you want to portray when you're out trolling the bar for boys (hard-to-get librarian) or impressing your girls (my bag is bigger than your bag), and you need to take the same kind of approach for the networking event. Whether it's a tradeshow, conference, or even hopping on a flight, because you're relying entirely on your look to make an impression and evoke come-hither attraction, you gotta have a plan. You're going to be surrounded by the masses in this kind of forum so the key is to think standout and conversation starter. Put on a mention-worthy piece of jewelry or slip into a vibrant color and watch 'em flock.

First date = interview

The guy on the other side of the table in either one of these instances is thinking one thing and one thing only: "Do we fit?" It's hard to hear, but the truth is there's a little bit of "Am I going to be proud to have this woman on my arm (team) or am I going to need to hide her?" involved. With limited get-to-know-you time, you've got to step up to the plate and make it easy on him. You wouldn't wear your tiara to a sports bar and this is certainly not the time to show off your concert shirt collection. Know both your environment and industry style expectations in advance. If you're unable to get a clear picture, always go for the overdress—it demonstrates respect and effort.

Meet the parents = client presentation

This can be a tough one because you don't always know what you're dealing with in advance and multiple parties are involved: the mom who doesn't want to see your cleavage, the dad who wants to believe his son is with a looker, the sister who wants to borrow your clothes. In the case of the "presentation," I believe in going strong, powerful, but primarily understated. Your presentation is what needs to speak volumes—not your hot pink miniskirt.

Day-to-day living together = the nine-to-five grind

When I get home from work, I can't jump into my lounge pants (holey pajamas) fast enough. Did I mention I'm divorced? Now I don't really think that's why the relationship didn't work, and no, you're not going to get fired for wearing your Juicy sweats three days in a row, but would a little bit of effort have brought more passion, energy, excitement to the situation? Yes. Of all the occasions we're talking about here, this is the one most worth mentioning (I'm guessing you're putting a little effort into the big meeting) because honestly—this is where it counts. Not only in how others perceive you (you've heard the dress-for-the-job-you-want expression) but also because of how dressing up makes you feel. I've done the test-drive many a time and I'm just that teensy bit smarter when wearing a dress. Just try it—for a week, wear your best (after work, too) and see what it does to your performance.

Devil Is in the Details

I have a good friend who's gorgeous . . . if you can get past the stray whiskers sprouting from her chin. The real secret in all this grooming stuff is that people don't necessarily notice when you're groomed, but they notice when you're not. I know it feels like a lot of effort for the little details, but this is where it counts.

Hair

I see so many beautifully dressed women who top it off with a mop of hair that seriously makes me think she should have stuck to the sweats. Here are some rules of thumb: The day is long, drag a brush through it; using mascara to cover your roots is for emergencies only (and preferably only when you're going to be seen at a distance). And what did your mom teach you about going outdoors with wet hair? And while we're on the topic of hair, if you're like my friend and have a 'stache, invest in laser hair removal. The best money you'll ever spend.

Teeth

I come from a family of bad bridgework. My own teeth have been ground, veneered, polished—you name it. Whatever option I'm given, I'll take it. Nothing says, "I grew up in a trailer" quite like a mouthful of yellow snaggleteeth. Keep that in mind when you're tempted to bail on your biannual cleaning.

Polish

An overcoat of shine or luster. How fantastic is that for a definition of polish? Who doesn't want to be lustrous? There are five areas in which you want to ensure you're applying polish:

✓ Nails

I know it's easier and cheaper in New York, but if you're going open toe, give them a coat.

✓ Shoes

Another pet peeve of mine. What's the use of wearing a rocking pair of stilettos if they're all banged up? It's so cheap to take them in to a shoe guy and have them polished and resoled—no excuses.

✓ Bag

The cobbler will take care of the outside of this baby as well but the innards are your responsibility. Nothing says disorganized like a bag full of scrap paper, loose makeup, and tampons.

✓ Posture

Ask your friends, family, coworkers to call you out every time they see you slouching—it's a habit you can break. Standing up straight has a tremendous impact on adding a little shine to any outfit. (Do I even need to mention it makes you look skinnier?)

✓ Manners

The most important element of all. You can be dressed to the nines and it's not going to matter if you're a rude bitch.

The Girl on Top Ten Commandments of Style

When it comes to style, some people just have piss poor taste. But there are some tried-and-true rules everyone should follow that will seriously reduce the frump running rampant in workplaces worldwide. Hang these up on your mirror, take them with you when shopping if you must, but never leave for work without having consulted the Girl on Top Ten.

1. **Know your body.** We're living in a society that encourages women to accept their bodies the way they are—which would be fabulous if we were all spawns of Victoria Beckham. Unfortunately, women take "embracing curves" to mean "wear whatever the hell you want" even if you've got rolls spilling over the sides of your jeans. When in doubt, go a size up. Even when you err on the side of too big, the clothing can still look tasteful, whereas going a size too tight leaves no hope for

those mornings after you've gorged on free wine and hors d'oeuvres at a client dinner. And remember, no one's too skinny for Spanx. If you haven't invested in quality shape wear yet, please do so *now*. Time is of the essence.

2. **Choose classic over trendy.** The same spellbound society that tells us our bodies are fine just the way they are also supports us in freely expressing our personal style—which again, would be great, if some of us didn't leave the house looking like a poor man's Pamela Anderson. Adding your own flare is great when we're talking about a necklace or a punchy-colored heel, but (especially if you work in a conservative atmosphere) save your trend experiments for the weekends. If you haven't studied fashion and you don't have a personal stylist, chances are your "risks" are actually mistakes—and therefore, not appreciated at the office.

3. **Fit trumps quality.** The rule has always been quality over quantity, but that's not completely true. The secret is that *fit* tops them both, always. Yes—it's entirely possible to look God-awful in Gucci. And as I said before, you can make an inexpensive outfit look like a million bucks if it's fitted (and forgiving) in all the right places. Plus, now that we have designers teaming with chain stores like Target and Kohl's, you can find good stuff on the cheap. The point is, where you get it should be second to how it looks on your body, which brings me to my next tip: If it ain't tailored, it ain't flattering. If you've never had a suit jacket or a pair of pants tailored, I cry a silent tear for what I fear you look like every morning when

you get to work. Muffin tops, peekaboo bra straps, butt cleavage, camel toe . . . I take that back—it's a full-on ugly cry. Not only might a tailor be the secret to all of your dating problems, but he has the power to catapult you to the corner office.

4. **Splurge when necessary (or keep the tags on!).** You're not likely to hear this advice from your financial advisor, but I've charged many a power suit to the credit card because I knew it would be just the look (and the confidence boost) I'd need to land a deal or ace an interview. There are certain times (and you'll recognize them when they happen) when looking your "usual best" just won't cut it. When you're presented with opportunities of a lifetime and you've got one chance to do it right, no price is too high to look the part. (And anyone who tries to tell you otherwise has never landed a major deal.)

5. **Mind your lines.** I never thought I'd say this, but Lindsay Lohan and Britney Spears have got something right—sort of. I'm not suggesting that you spare visible panty lines at *any* price, but you can—and should—find your way around them. With all the different kinds of undies available, there's just no excuse.

6. **Black is always back.** And so is gray or navy blue, which can be less harsh with some skin tones and hair color, but is still equally clean, sleek, and slimming. When it comes to color, you want to wear your clothes, not have them wear you. A punch of color is one thing; a canary yellow ensemble for a

first interview is another. At the end of the day you want them to remember you and your presentation, not, "You know . . . what's her name . . . big yellow."

7. **Good shoes can transform an outfit.** Although you may be able to fake expensive with clothing, with shoes, you get what you pay for. No, seriously—wear Payless, and you can actually expect to be paid less. On the other hand, you could be sporting an entire outfit from Forever 21 and still look spectacular if your feet are in a pair of Manolos. And while I don't recommend shopping for clothing online (for fear of fit being sacrificed), shoes are a much safer bet. Shopbob, Bluefly, and Zappos are all great sites for designer shoes at the click of a mouse. So now that I've given you the permission you've been waiting for . . . start saving!

8. **Accessorize in moderation.** Jewelry can be your outfit's best friend or its worst enemy. A few guidelines to follow: If you're going with a statement piece (a striking necklace or a bold cocktail ring), go bare to minimal elsewhere. And unless you've been lent a Swarovski set to go with your red carpet gown, there should be no matching of the earrings, bracelets, and necklaces—too much of one thing screams "I shop at Claire's." As far as other accessories go—the bag draped over your arm, the scarf tied around the neck, the belt cinching your waist—you can go cheap on all but the bag. Clients, coworkers, interviewers—whether you believe it or not, they're all sizing up your game by what you're packing.

9. **Learn how to layer.** Layering gone wrong turns even the slimmest of women into lumpy, disproportioned mishaps. If there's one combination that's essential to master, it's the meeting-to-work-to-I-need-a-drink-ASAP arrangement. The trick is to start with the thinnest and tightest layer underneath (like a dress, a sexy cami, or a fitted tee), add a slightly chunkier layer (a cardigan or a knit sweater), and then throw a blazer on top of it all. Get it right and you'll transition seamlessly from early morning to late night without ever having to fear the walk of shame. Some more hints on layering: Swap in pieces from different seasons underneath to get more out of your wardrobe, and stick to one pattern per combo.

10. **Turn to the experts.** People think style is a gene you're either born with or not. But even the fashionistas of the world have been caught looking like shit at one point or another. The fact of the matter is that they practice looking good, and they get better at it as they become more attuned to what accommodates their tastes and flatters their figures. I get that so many women don't have the time or the energy to invest in learning to look their best. But for the sake of your career—and the rest of us who subconsciously judge you—seek help. Ask a fashionable friend to raid your closet or hire a stylist for a single consultation. Sign up for my "WORKS style" newsletter for weekly work wardrobe recommendations. And finally, take advantage of stores with free shopping services such as Bloomingdales, Saks, J.Crew, and Club Monaco. It's a small

investment of time and the payoff—a newfound sense of confidence—is worth it.

Okay, so after all that, the truth is if you come across an ass who doesn't like you . . . promote you . . . hire you, because they don't dig your looks—it's *their* problem, not yours.

Chapter 10

Get a Life

If you're after success, you need to put out. You'll be put in positions you've only dreamed of. You will be asked to deliver on a level you never thought possible. You will feel exposed, exhausted, and exhilarated. Hard work is the name of the game. But here's the thing. There is this very critical point at which all of your self-sacrifice starts to feel like just that—the sacrifice of your "self." And this is where you're in the danger zone. Lose yourself and you've lost everything.

I've drawn inspiration for this chapter from the way-too-many women I come across who, after giving up everything for the sake of their career, wear bitterness like a badge. In each and every one of these cases she's led herself to believe one of three big, fat lies:

He can't survive without me

I'm all about working your ass off to become indispensable, but at the end of the day . . . you're not. When you mistakenly believe that you are your job and that your job can only be performed by you and you alone, you move into this place of possession and control that is (a) so not fun (can't meet your girls for drinks when you're the only one who can turn out the lights) and (b) prevents you from moving on to something bigger and better. Take the night off. I promise, they *will* survive.

I'm doing this all for him

Now be honest with yourself. Are you doing this for the boss or are you doing this so that your boss gives you attention and sympathy? The difference between working hard and being the martyr is entirely distinguished by objective. Killing yourself for a clear and defined objective that leads to your (and her) advancement is called hard work. Knocking yourself out as a means to an end is called martyrdom. Letting everyone know that you are clocking more hours than Movado is like FTDing yourself on Valentine's Day— kinda pathetic. No one likes a martyr . . . not even the boss who expects you to do whatever it takes to get the job done.

When he/they/I _____ . . .

This is the classic. When I (fill in the blank), then I will take the vacation, have a kid, call my mom. I'm actually watching a good friend of mine live this in a personal relationship and her blank is: when he <u>leaves her</u>. In the meantime, she's put her life on hold waiting for this momentous occasion to arrive. Time goes by way too quickly to put your whole life on hold waiting for your kids to grow up, for him to come to his senses, or for the big CEO title. With any luck at all you'll never be done "arriving," and in the meantime there's a lot of life to live.

Keep Things Interesting

Beyond the fact that you don't want to look like a loser with no life outside the office, there are a lot of good reasons why it's important to get a life. Just like a man, your career requires that you have outside stimulation, support, and inspiration to keep things interesting.

Bring something to the table

The only way you're going to keep the fire alive is to get out from under your job and expose yourself to new people and circumstances. Take a class, volunteer, become a bungee jumper. Just do *something* that doesn't involve your office.

Believe that absence makes the heart grow fonder

Seriously, you'd get sick of George Clooney if you had to live with him each and every day. (Well, maybe not, but the point is . . .) I don't care how much you love your job—we all need a break. A chance to get away and not only have your boss appreciate all you have to offer, but allow you to remember why you fell in love with it in the first place.

Don't be a monkey on her back

You'd think this wouldn't apply to your career, but the same way your beau doesn't appreciate the pressure of being your whole life, neither does your boss. Of course she wants you to be present and accounted for, but the pressure of "this girl is nothing without me" isn't what she's after.

Have other, better options

How are you ever going to know what else is out there if you're chained to your desk 24/7? One of the most dangerous side effects of burying yourself in your work is to believe that not only are there no other options, but that this is the *best* one you've got.

Get Over Yourself

Yeah, I know. Your world is filled with people who suck the life out of you. I need this, give me that . . . it's a familiar tune. But guess what? There are people out there with much bigger problems than yours. And no matter how tired you are, or how much your boss pissed you off, knowing that something you did benefited someone else is bound to make you feel better. Here are some other ways volunteering can help you, um, I mean them.

It makes you look good. Not buying it? Well, consider Angelina Jolie. She went from a freakishly weird goth chick who made out with her brother and wore a vial of her husband's blood around her neck, to a modern-day Mother Teresa. Instead of the paparazzi chronicling her every coffee run, they follow her to far-flung places where she helps the poor and adopts abandoned children. Not bad PR if you can get it. Don't fail to mention you've been representing a good cause, come review time.

It's like a singles bar sans the sweaty losers. The majority of do-gooding happens at great venues and attracts dynamic, successful people. Charity events are loaded with smart single (or married but well-connected) men who clearly have a sensitive side. Not only will you instantly have something to talk about (your shared commitment to clean air), but if your organization holds weekly meetings, that's guaranteed get-to-know-you time.

It gives you the chance to try out a new skill. Maybe you're terrible at planting trees, or couldn't get someone to give you a donation if you offered to make it for them, but volunteering gives you the chance to test your talents without pressure. After all, they aren't paying you to be there, so they're not expecting you to raise a million your first go-round.

It makes you realize you aren't the center of the universe. There have been a lot of times in building my business when I was sick and tired of trying. I wanted to quit. Wanted to leave this all behind and find a cottage somewhere and milk goats. (Can you actually milk a goat??) Anyway, always, just when I'm about to give up, I meet someone for whom this business matters. Career success requires perseverance, a willingness to push the limit, a commitment, and at the end of the day, there's going to have to be something in it for more than just you.

R&R—Request and Response

You may want a life but your boss isn't so sure. Like that guy who's more of a booty call than a boyfriend, here are some clear indicators that you're being taken advantage of—and how to stop it.

The Request

A member of senior management—who isn't your direct superior—asks you to do her expense report and then proceeds to dump three months of receipts on your desk.

Your Response

Explain that while you'd love to help her sort out her expense account, you have to cater to your own boss's needs first. Hello, doesn't she have her own assistant?

The Request

You helped your boss address her sister's baby shower invitations because she was desperate. Now she wants you to write the thank-you notes, too.

Your Response

Ask her if she'd like you to do the thank-you notes instead of working on her client presentation. Hopefully she'll get the hint that you've got real work to do.

The Request

You volunteer to cover for your coworker while he's out on vacation—and then realize he hasn't touched most of his accounts in at least three months.

Your Response

Tell him that while you don't mind covering, you can't do his job for him. You have enough of your own work to worry about.

The Request

Your coworker asks you to order him a sandwich from the place you're getting lunch from, then "forgets" to give you money to pay the delivery guy.

Your Response

Tell him that while you wish you could afford to spring for lunch, your salary hardly covers your own food. Then wait at his desk until he coughs up the cash.

Back to Life

I'm watching (enviously) as one of my new friends is in the throes of new love. She disappears for weekends at a time (unheard of), thinks his head tic thing is adorable (it's not), and can talk of nothing but how sensitive he is (*zzzzzz*). In about six weeks (after she finally gives her head a shake) she'll be coming back to her life (own apartment) wondering where we're going Saturday night (our regular).

Infatuation: It's easy to see from the outside, but oh so difficult to recognize when we're enraptured. For me, it's often less about a new guy and more about a new project, but on more than one occasion

I've returned from the 24/7 abyss to find friends and family are pissed and my dog has reverted to hunting and gathering.

When you finally come down from the grappling high that goes with a new engaging project at work, it's time to make amends and reconnect with your out-of-office life. Set aside electronic-free time with those you've forgotten about and follow a few rules:

Give them a heads-up

It can catch you by surprise, but if you know in advance you're going undercover, explain what you're up to and why it's so important to you. That'll stop them from putting your picture on a milk carton advertisement for the missing—or sending you "Are you alive?" e-mails. And if all goes well, your friends and family will be excited for your new venture and they'll feel less resentful upon your return.

Say thanks

As soon as you've reemerged, get out the pen and paper. (Save the Facebook status updates and the mass e-mails for later.) Sometimes all it takes to set something right is a little apology and appreciation. Write a heartfelt note thanking your peeps for standing by you and let them know how excited you are to catch up with their lives. Then make sure when they do call, you answer.

Bite your tongue

You had your turn; now it's theirs so get ready to listen. As much as you'd like to go on and on about all of your successes (and how hard you work for them), keep a lid on it. No mention of that four-letter word (w-o-r-k). Let them do the talking.

Do You Need to Get a Life?

It's hard to know that you don't have one when you don't have one. Here are a few signs:

- ❑ Your eyes have forgotten how to adjust to natural daylight.
- ❑ Peeing is a setback.
- ❑ Walking to the photocopier and back totally counts as exercise.
- ❑ The people framed on your desk are giving you the middle finger.
- ❑ When your mother calls, you tell her you've got a "hard stop" at eight.
- ❑ You interrupt sex to check your BlackBerry.
- ❑ You stop flushing the toilet at home because you forget it's not automatic.
- ❑ You lecture the delivery guy on how his tardiness affects the bottom line.
- ❑ Your favorite way to relax is to organize your e-mail correspondence.
- ❑ You sign texts to friends with "Best," and "I look forward to our reconvening."
- ❑ The dude in accounting with the spitting problem has started to look delicious.

Chapter 11

Don't Give Away
Your Milk for Free

O nce upon a time there was a brilliant, gorgeous, witty princess (employee) who gave her heart and soul to her beloved prince (boss). In the hopes of getting a marriage proposal (promotion), she did everything she could to please him (worked her ass off) and never asked anything in return (for free). One day, his right-hand stable boy asked, "Why don't you buy the cow?"

His response: "Why, when I can get the milk for free?"

Of all the dating rules I pulled for this book, this is the classic. For centuries, mothers around the globe have been encouraging their little girls to hold out for a commitment and with good reason—it works. Let me lay it out for you:

- In any situation where you are looking for an offer (marriage, raise, job, promotion) there needs to be a "price" for the exchange.
- The price is a two-way street. There's a cost for making the offer (a job, ring, money) and a cost for not making the offer (you walking over to the competition).
- And here's the clincher: The price of you walking away (not making the offer) needs to be higher (more painful) than the price attached to enticing you to stay.

Whether it's your beau or your boss, if you want to get anything out of the relationship, you have to have a handle on three things: how to set, negotiate, and get your price.

How Much Do You Cost?

Don't kid yourself, we all have a price. One of the worst mistakes you can make is to sit back and let others define what you're worth in the marketplace—what you're willing to live with and what you can't live without. You're certainly going to seek feedback and inspiration from others. And sure, your price is going to change over time, but the bottom line is that setting your price is something you need to do for yourself. If you don't feel well compensated, you'll be resentful every time a client or colleague gives you something to do. Definitely not a recipe for success—yours or theirs.

Set Your Price

Price is defined as the cost for which something is obtained. Why I like this definition is that the "cost" refers to a transaction. Of course, there is more to a career opportunity to consider than just the hard cold cash (passion, relationships, an opportunity to influence and do good by others, flexibility), but for most women, this is the hardest line to draw in the sand. It can be difficult to put a price on ourselves but it's absolutely necessary. What's it going to take to buy your brilliance?

- **Get a handle on the numbers.** Your future employer will already know them, and so should you. The good news is that there is a lot of information out there to help you find a negotiating point. After you've added your income goal to your cost of living, and considered your geographic location, check it against these resources:
  - The Bureau of Labor Statistics' *Occupational Outlook Handbook*
  - Salary.com
  - *Salary Facts Handbook*

  Or if you're feeling really ballsy, you can ask people in the industry how much they make, especially friends who've left their jobs to have kids or have made a career change. Now that they aren't in it—read: not competing with you anymore— they'll be more likely to tell you the truth. But seriously this method should be reserved for close friends and family only. It's kinda like asking, "So, how much did the ring set him back?"

- **Accentuate the positive.** We've all got our faults, but price-setters are able to keep them in the shadows by highlighting their strengths. So what if you're not exactly a clean freak? Your killer lasagna and animalistic libido will make him forget all about the dirty dishes piling up in the sink. Your task is to make a case that your best attributes are the most important for the job. Lay out what you're good at.

- **Command a premium.** Maybe it's 10 percent, maybe it's 20 percent—depends on the industry, your experience, and how brave you are. The point is you'll need to argue that you're worth more than the masses. If you've got the skills, knowl-edge, training, and reputation, go ahead and bump it up. You teach your guy how to treat you by setting a standard of what you will and won't tolerate—the same goes in business. If you show that you value yourself, people are more likely to con-sider a price closer to what you've asked for. And remember: The worst thing they can say is no.

- **Stretch the truth.** If you're on a job interview and a potential employer asks you what you're current salary is, now's not the time to be honest. Bump it up 10 or 15 percent. I always assume that someone has increased what they're making to give us ne-gotiation room. Just don't go overboard. Doubling your salary or asking for a ballsy perk (like a car service to work every morning) will get you laughed out of his office—especially in a shitty economy.

Trick of the Trade: Honesty Is the Only Policy
(at least with yourself)

In order to set your price, you need to be honest with yourself. If you want a ring, you want a ring. If you want be famous, you want to be famous. If you want to retire at thirty to have kids, you want to retire at thirty to have kids. You can't set your price without knowing what it is you want in the grand scheme of things. A lot of women tell me they don't know what they want . . . but they do—they're just too afraid or too embarrassed or shy to put it out there. Whether you say it out loud or keep it to yourself, be honest about what you're after. It's the key to not only setting your price but having a better handle on what you're willing to sacrifice in order to get it.

Negotiating Your Price

Unless you want to buy your own engagement ring or write your own paycheck, there is a whole other step in this cow-buying process. Your price is a transactional figure, and while it needs to be determined first in your own mind, it means nothing without creating value. And in order for something to have value, someone has to be willing to buy it. In an ideal world what we're selling and what they're buying are exactly allied, but that's rarely the case. Whether you're negotiating for a new job or asking for a raise, what you need to do is negotiate a compromise. And here's how:

Put it on the table

Your boss is not a mind reader. You've got to make your price known.

Time it right

The longer you wait and give yourself away for free, the harder it is to seal the deal. Not only does he get accustomed to the way things are, he's going to resent being pressured to ante up.

Simmer down

I'm all about expressing yourself with passion and with a level of firmness, but try and steer clear of becoming a raging lunatic. Heading into the crazies will only make him wonder if this is really what he wants to get himself into.

Listen and learn

Believe it or not, it's not all about you. He also has a price. Once you've communicated what your intentions are for the relationship, you need to stop talking and hear what it is that he's after. You may not be as far away from an agreement as you thought, or you may be going at it all wrong. Either way, you're not going to get what you want without hearing and understanding his bottom line.

Give to get

I've been learning a lot about negotiating lately and one of the more interesting things is that often it's not simply about the money (or the corner office . . . or the proposal), but about many of the things that come with it. Things like loyalty (nondisclosure), commitment (noncompetes), and opportunity (bonus). The more willing you are to give, the more you tend to get.

The Other Negotiables

Maybe a raise is the ultimate goal, but there are some other options you can ask for that are just as valuable when added up. Think of it like foreplay—not as much pressure involved, and yet the payoff can be equally rewarding

BlackBerry. It costs approximately $960 per year to keep you well
   connected. You may not have any excuses for being unavailable,
   but at least you can get *US Weekly* updates any time of day.

Transportation reimbursement. Comparable to a $1,300 raise
   if you take the subway once each way; or about $360 per year
   if you drive around ten miles to work. Who said nothing good
   ever comes from a free ride?

One day a week from home. An extra hour of your time to
   spend productively, a break on transportation costs, and an
   escape from your bitch of a boss . . . What's it worth to you?

Gym membership. It won't reflect so well on the company when
   your fat ass can't squeeze into the client's conference room chair.
   For an extra $600 to $1,000 you'll be in top performing shape.

Health insurance. A big cost for freelancers, health insurance can
   cost $300 to $500 per month at the most basic level. Ask them
   to comp it and that's $3,600 to $6,000 more in your pocket.

Time off. Say you make $50,000 a year—that's $137 dollars a day. Negotiate an extra week of paid time off and you're worth $685 more than you were yesterday.

Laptop. Approximately $800—not a bad bonus. Even better, no more reason to be at the office past six . . . Suckers!

Education. A single seminar, a night class, an entire MBA . . . The cost to the employer can run the gamut, but to you the value of education (and scoring the professor's digits) can open doors you'd never imagined.

Environmental friendliness. Carpooling, biking to work, converting to a paperless file system . . . Some companies offer bonuses for complying with green guidelines or for developing more ecofriendly systems. Thinner thighs? No paperwork? Once you go green, you never go back.

Give 'Em a Little Taste

Sure there are times you need to whet their whistle, but the key is not filling him so full he never needs or wants to drink again. There's a fine line between what's free and what's not.

- **Free:** You offer to critique or be a sounding board for a new marketing strategy.
- **Not free:** You create and implement said strategy.

- **Free:** You make one last-minute change to a project for him.
- **Not free:** You make ten changes.

- **Free:** You give her new novel a read before she sends it to an agent.
- **Not free:** You write her novel for her.

- **Free:** You work a couple of hours of overtime and don't bill her.
- **Not Free:** You work forty hours of overtime and don't bill her.

- **Free:** You mock up a project so he can see your style and aesthetic.
- **Not free:** You make repeated changes to the mock up before he's agreed to hire you.

Getting Your Way

I know this sounds overly simplistic but I promise you the quickest, most effective way of getting what you want is your willingness (regardless of how badly you want it) to walk away. If the threat of you taking your talented, brilliant, gorgeous self over to the competitor isn't enough to make him wrap his arms around you and give you what you want . . . he's not that into you.

Chapter 12

Don't Waste the Pretty

They can't find the budget? Stellar interview but they've decided to outsource the position? Not returning your calls? Yeah, he's just not that into you. Here's the truth: For the right person there's always more money, an opening, a call back. Don't waste the pretty.

I know a lot of women in their late thirties and early forties who are pissed for having stuck it out with the wrong guy for way too long. Yes, of course you can both find love and create a kick-ass career into your fifties, sixties, and beyond, but let's be frank: There are only so many optimal, peak-performance years you've got to work with and I don't want you wasting your prime with a jackass of a boss who doesn't appreciate all you have to offer.

As your mom promised . . . there are plenty of fish in the sea.

Could Be Worse, Right?

Fear of hurting your feelings, bigger fish to fry, the holidays are around the corner, they haven't found the right person to fill your spot—for whatever reason, your boss isn't willing to pull the trigger and make the break. It's not like he's cruel, or you'd walk on out the door. Rather, it's a kind of complacency that lulls you into thinking "It could be worse" when, in reality, what's worse than being led to believe that there's something worth hanging around for . . . when there isn't? It wastes your time, your energy, your life. If he's not big enough to admit he hasn't got his heart in it, here are the signs that you need to be the one who cuts the cord.

No review

Even if it isn't stellar and there's some work to be done to improve your performance, feedback is a critical indicator that he's invested. It's the same way you can tell if your boyfriend's still in it for the long haul. He wouldn't bother to suggest new ways of doing things if he didn't think there'd be a next time. So if it's been weeks, months, years since you've gotten any good (or bad) reviews, take it as a sign. And don't think that it's because he's forgotten—he hasn't. It's just that, like the rest of us, he hates to deliver bad news and he's simply delaying the inevitable.

No rewards

The suggestion of a day off, a spa gift certificate, having his driver take you home after staying late, a birthday card—even if a big bonus isn't in the budget, you should be getting a little something extra for your efforts. Ever notice how a man's all eager to shower you with gifts at the beginning of your relationship? Then, as the honeymoon fades, so do the subtle paybacks. Though you're probably not sleeping with your boss (although if you are, this rule applies twice over), he still owes you reciprocation. So if he hasn't sweetened the pot to keep you enticed, bet your bottom dollar there's someone else he's sinking his teeth into.

No relations

The telltale sign that you're just not doing it for your boss? No introductions. He won't invite you to meetings with new clients, he doesn't ask you to charm the vendors, and he definitely keeps you clear of his boss's boss. When a guy is into you, he'll show you off—take you to parties, invite you home for the holidays, and he'll most certainly want to be seen with you in public. If he's not eager to brag, you're either on your way out or he's two-timing you with someone who's about to fill your shoes.

No reservations

Eating with someone is a private, primitive act of trust building that dates back to the caveman. So much can be learned about people over dinner—the way they were raised, their level of taste, their consideration for others . . . An entire intimate conversation can be had when sharing food without a word being uttered. The point is, if he's into you, he'll invest the time and money to get to know you better in the context of a drink or a meal. Even the most reclusive of bosses won't keep you chained at your desk eating take-out forever.

No responsibility

It would be just fine with him if you came strolling in past two every night. Oh, and you forgot to call? That's okay, too—no sweat off his back. As unconditional as that sounds, a guy who never holds you accountable for your wrongdoings just doesn't give a shit. Likewise, a boss who strips you of your responsibilities or never trusts you with any real ones in the first place is only keeping you around until he finds better.

No room

Okay, you are a star performer. You beat your numbers every month, and you're still sharing a cubicle with your lazy assistant who has an audio-enabled screen saver of her cat's most glamorous snapshots. People at your level in other departments have real offices, with four solid walls and a door to slam. Or at least they have their own cubicle without a gum-snapping, tune-humming maniac who retrieves her voicemail via speakerphone. You don't have a window, but the summer intern does? You're on top of the heating vent so you sweat through your Theory suit, even in February? You might have a great title, which looks impressive as hell at a client meeting, but where you sit shows what your boss really thinks of you. He's sending you a message, and the message is "move on."

Turning the Tides in Your Favor

The shock of someone not digging you at the office can be even worse than being rejected at the bar—it's not like they have to pick just one. I've seen grown women driven to distraction, resorting to some clearly love-crazed-like actions in the hopes of winning the nonsupporter over. If leaving's not an option and you don't want to make a bad situation worse, follow these steps:

Let her come to you

We've covered this ad nauseam but think reverse psychology. Pretend you could care less (preferably make it true) and she'll come running to you. Kinda like children and animals, the more you want to play, the more you put them off. Back off and give her some space.

Be the most popular

Just like any hot-blooded, competitive guy is going to reconsider his decision to dump you once he sees you with your new (preferably taller, hotter, smarter, richer) beau, your nemesis is going to second-guess her opinion once she witnesses your colleagues (preferably more senior to her) lapping you up. Even if she still has a hate-on for you, she's going to give you the necessary distance and respect for fear of ruffling any feathers.

Ask the question . . .

"How would you handle this situation?" It's a rare breed who isn't swayed by the vanity of not only being asked to share her opinion, but her experience. The trick is you have to get the phrasing just right for this one or you'll sound like a kiss-ass and make her hate you even more.

The last resort

I offer this one up with a word of caution. As your very last resort, come out with it and ask, "Do you have a problem with me?" The risk is that she didn't—until now, when she realizes you're a loser. The only reason I think it's worth the risk (especially for those of you who have a lot of haters) is that while you may lose the battle (her affection forever), you could win the war (finally figure out what you're doing wrong). There are so many fantastically talented women out there who would have so many more people into them if they only had that knowledge.

Why He's Not That Into You

So I'm scared. I keep meeting the same woman. She's in her early to mid-forties. She has a dog or multiple cats. She had a significant relationship in her early thirties that she gave up in the hope of something more . . . he still hasn't arrived. She's considering either insemination or adoption. She's angry and can't for the life of her figure out why she's still single. (Hint, hint: Your desperation is palpable and makes every living creature want to get the hell away from you.)

I've known this woman (bitter, it's-everyone-else-who-is-the-problem, entitled, rude) in the career space for years now, but as I stand, teetering on the edge of becoming the single, barren, angry girl with the dog, I have newfound incentive for telling the cold, hard truth about why he's just not that into you:

You're a smarty pants

I'm actually working with a woman who has this disease. I'll offer a new perspective (she did hire me for my expertise) and she interjects with: "I know . . . I know . . . I know."

Hint, hint: You don't *know* and you won't ever *know* because you don't listen. The reason why you're not getting ahead in your career is that you're not smart enough to shut your mouth and learn something new. And that condescending little attitude of yours? Makes people want to push you down. Good luck to ya!

You're a blamer

You know this woman—she's the one who believes her lack of success has everything to do with her parents' divorce, the fact that she couldn't afford to go to Harvard (or get accepted for that matter), and that her ex-boyfriend's girlfriend called her boss to sabotage her chance at the promotion.

Hint, hint: Yeah, so here's the deal. Not everyone is out to get you. In fact, you're so into conspiracy theories that you don't even show up on the radar. No one cares enough about you to waste their time taking you down. You and only you are responsible for the fact that you're going nowhere fast.

You're on a high horse

I don't do coffee.

Hint, hint: Oh yes you do and with a smile on your face. Your title is assistant and you've clocked a whopping three weeks. We're a team here, and if you're asked to jump, the only acceptable response is, "How high?" Give flack on the little things, and you're never going to be asked to do the big things.

You're a martyr

Please, please, please don't become this woman—she's the one who's given up everything (read: husband, kids, happiness) in order to get the job done and no one—I mean no one—gives a shit.

Hint, hint: The fact that you're at the office 'til eleven every single night isn't something to be proud of. In fact, we all pretty much think you're a loser and are using you as a model of who we don't want to become. I'm all for working hard but the trick is *not* to talk about it. If you really do bust your ass, let other people make the observation. And then once they comment on how hard you work, you respond, "It's nothing."

Don't Waste Your Pretty

Not wasting the pretty is a two-way street, and there are a few people at the office who you need not be into:

The slacker: Give her an inch and she'll take the proverbial mile. You've got your own job to do, and while we're not suggesting you throw her lazy ass under the bus, picking up her slack is only furthering one career—and it's not yours.

The office bike: Everyone's taken a ride, and you don't want to know the juicy details.

The leech: This one will suck you dry if you let her. Let's get lunch, let's get drinks, let's sit next to each other at every freakin' meeting. Get out while you can.

The drunk: Sure she's the life of the party, but if you get branded her sidekick, people will begin to think you like your liquor as much as she does—whether that be true or not. There's no harm in wanting to have fun, but do it with your friends, not your coworkers.

The bully: It's like the elementary school playground all over again, only this time you know that the bully is really just an insecure, miserable person who gets off on making others feel as bad as he does. Let him know you won't take his shit. Then don't.

Chapter 13

Lay Off the Liquor

T his is the one rule you'd think would be so obvious it wouldn't be worth mentioning but I want you to pull out this page, put it in your wallet, and the next time you sidle up to the bar with colleagues and pull out your credit card to start a tab, read it again. *Lay off the liquor.* No one likes a drunk—they're sloppy, high-maintenance, have loose lips— it's embarrassing, and unlike your friends and family, your colleagues really do need to respect you in the morning.

Business lunches, drinks after work, charity dinners—these are amazing opportunities for you to build relationships and create success. With that in mind, I'm going to lay out everything you need to know about social dining, networking, and drinking—when it's important to order a drink and when it's important not to.

Everything in Moderation

So after scaring you into sobriety (as if), I'm not saying that you can't take advantage of that one glass of courage-enhancing wine. What I am saying is that you've gotta know your limit and, even more important, stick to it. Too many drinks and you threaten your credibility faster than you can utter, "'Nother round!" Here are some baseline rules:

Know when to fold 'em

Having parents who turned a blind eye to the occasional beer-steal, by the time I got to college I had experienced my fair share of room-spinning, vomit-inducing, nonrecollection of boy-kissing experiences. Nevertheless the first time I came home to see my roommate peeing in the corner of our room, I was a little surprised. The key to having a drink, or even two, is knowing your limit. And the office holiday party is not where you want to test it out. If you haven't tested your tolerance in a while, give the girls a call.

Do not keep up with the boys

Yeah, they're usually weighing in at a solid fifty to eighty pounds heavier than you are, so no, not a good idea to go one for one. This is one instance where you want to forgo the competition with the boys.

A time for everything

I was trying out a new diet that required I abstain from alcohol, when I learned just how delicate the balance of joining a beau or colleague for a drink really is. The issue is that if it's just the two of you and he wants a drink, it makes him feel a little judged if you decline. You know what they say about the dude who drinks alone. You can either order a drink and take a sip, leaving the rest behind (he really does have a problem if he asks if you're done with that before reaching across the table), or just say you wish you could, but can't.

No roadies

Don't even think about drinking and driving. Career suicide. It's game over if you're dead or God forbid you kill someone, but don't overlook the fact that many companies run a criminal record check, and yes, the DUI you got when you're twenty-two is still on there.

Why Not

We've covered how to have a drink or two, but now let's be crystal clear why three is a bad idea. What I'm worried about is you knocking back one too many glasses of champagne, only to vomit, dance like a fool, be carried out of the bar, or roll over to find your boss. The thing about drinking is that while you're doing it, you think you're the bomb, but you're not. It's called intoxication for a reason—you're out of your mind. All you need to do to remedy yourself of the "one too many drinks" syndrome is to hit the town sober . . . and observe the following shit-faced signs.

Loose lips

Alcohol opens the floodgates, and while immediately it feels good, it ultimately impedes rational thought and behavior. What starts as some fun-filled banter with your colleagues quickly slides into "You're an ass and everyone thinks so." Whether it's way too intimate information about you—or others—loose lips sink careers. Liquor has a way of lulling you into showing your true colors and no one really cares (or agrees) that you're the only one holding the company together or that you'd like to (or worse, just did) slap Emily upside the face.

Just plain loose

Get a couple of drinks in you and it's not just your lips that become loose. After slipping on the beer goggles, Ralph from accounting (whom you've never noticed before in your life) looks delicious and you decide to take him home for dessert. Enough said.

Mirror, mirror on the wall

I'm going to appeal to the vanity in all of us. When going out for the evening, have you ever left the apartment with one last look in the mirror and thought, "Pretty good"? And then hours, and many drinks, later, headed to the bathroom, snatched a peek, and wondered, "What happened?" Here's what happened: Drinking makes you ugly.

The Morning After

If you didn't heed my advice and had one too many, the remedies for hangover recovery on a Sunday are the same on a Tuesday, only with a few caveats.

First and foremost it's all about prevention. If, come eleven, you're having a blast and you know you're going down for the count, start to hydrate and set your BlackBerry alarm for two hours before you need to get up. You'll want to die when the bells go off, but get up, down a huge glass of water and a couple of Ibuprofen, and I promise you'll at least be functional at the office.

And the office is exactly where you need to be regardless of how shitty you feel. Don't even dream about calling in sick if either (a) you told *anyone* at the office you were going out on the town or (b) there's a chance in hell that someone (client, colleagues, vendors) from work may have caught sight of you knocking back the Patrón. Which really means, unless you're heading to the ER, get to work.

And when you finally hit the watercooler, keep your mouth shut. It's not attractive on the morning after to regale the highlights of the night before. This is especially true if you were out with colleagues, and even more so if you made an ass of yourself. In college it may have been fun to say, "And remember when I got on the bar," but you're not in college anymore, Toto. Be a big girl and suck it up.

Dining for Dollars

The two most lucrative offers of my life came over a meal. Somewhere between the bread basket and the bowl of steaming pasta (in both cases . . . love the carbs), I was offered a business partnership and a 5-carat diamond engagement ring. Not by the same guy, and I took one and not the other (let's hope I chose right). Beyond the need for sustenance, meals offer an occasion around which to make announcements, negotiate offers, and create an unprecedented opportunity to get to know you. While not all meals are created equal, the rules of the table are always the same.

Breakfast: Not ready to commit

The equivalent of meeting someone for coffee; usually a safe first date option because it represents the least commitment, from both a budget and a time standpoint. People want to get a move on with their day so breakfast meetings are usually the shortest—not the best time to order a three-course meal . . . or a drink.

Lunch: Get to know you

More like a Wednesday night or second date; things are a little more serious but you're still feeling things out. While longer than a breakfast date and shorter than dinner, it is still the least relaxed dining experience because you're typically rushing from and then back to the office—consider having a snack beforehand so you can spend more time talking instead of eating.

Dinner: Moving into serious territory

You've finally scored what is most like a Saturday night or third date. As in the dating world, dinner is typically a long time to spend with someone and the expectation is to close the deal! You can follow your date's lead and order a drink, but be wary that conversation is usually more personal over a few drinks. You can let your guard down a bit, but it's still not the place to praise your new vibrator—be respectful of maintaining appropriate boundaries— which is tough when you're drunk.

It won't matter if you're mowing down a bagel or a steak, if you don't mind your manners, the offer won't make its way over the table. Unless you were raised by wolves, I'm assuming you grew up with some table manners. But I get it, even I end up in situations where I'm like "What would Miss Manners do?" Over a high-stakes dinner, entrées hit the table and my guest needed to find the loo. Ten minutes and a lukewarm steak later, I'm thinking, "Good God, can I dig in?" (At twenty minutes I decided oh yes I can.) While certain situations require best guesses, there are some firm rules of the table.

After you

If your lunch date is a man, chances are he'll let you order first. That whole chivalry thing and all. If you're both women, the person who's paying (or is more superior in position) should go first. Use this as a guide to what you should order. If she gets an appetizer or a glass of wine, feel free to have one, too.

Would you care for coffee?

Of course you would, but if your lunch date is already on the Black-Berry, politely decline and hit up the coffee shop on the way back to your office.

Pick your poison

It's fine to order a glass of wine at lunch—especially if your date does first, but anything harder than that and you run the risk of looking like a lush. (The three-martini lunch is so 1975.) Stick to soda, water, or coffee.

Picking up the tab

One of the most awkward moments of a first date is when the bill arrives. Does he reach for it? (Um, he better if he wants to see you again.) Do you offer to pay your share? (Yes, you should at least offer.) The same is true for a business meal, especially since it can go so horribly wrong. The general rule is that if you're the one who invited the person out, expect to pick up the tab. But that can be tricky if that person is senior to you. Some people (the old school types who wouldn't be caught dead without wearing hose . . . in August) get all up in arms if you try to pay. They see getting the check as a power play—the one with the gold rules—and a neo-phyte like you needs to know her place.

This is a true story from a friend of mine: Several years ago she and her boss were meeting clients for drinks. The boss asked my friend to go on ahead because she was running late, and when the waitress asked for a credit card to start the tab, she readily handed over her Visa. At the end of the evening, when it came time to pay the bill, my friend told the waitress it was fine to put it on her card. The boss turned to her with a look of sheer territorial rage and spit out, "You're putting this on your card? No, we'll put it on mine." This was in front of the clients, who sat there looking like they'd rather be at an Ashley Simpson concert than watch the whole scene go down. The next day she was reprimanded for being insubordinate.

Now that boss clearly had some insecurity issues, but it brings up an interesting point. When you're out with a senior member of your firm, just follow their lead. It's so not worth fighting over who forks over for the foie gras. But when a junior staffer asks to take you out for coffee because she wants your advice, it's fine to let her spring for your skim latte. Your time's valuable. And one cup of coffee isn't going to put her in the poor house.

Then there are those times when the staff hits happy hour after work. You're the boss—they work hard—so you throw down your card and open a tab. Three hours—and $300—later, they're still going strong? At that point, you need to cut them off, or at least let them know that their next vodka tonic is on them. They'll be too wasted to care.

Chapter 14

Keep It Brief

I t really is a spectacle to behold. Land yourself in any bar on a
Saturday night and you can catch this one for yourself. From
across the room, she's looking at him . . . he's looking at her.
She's laughing, her head thrown back, running her fingers
through her hair. He lowers his chin, makes eye contact. She lifts
her glass and feigns a toast. He moves in. They pull their tables . . .
chairs . . . bodies together. She's drinking. They're kissing. He's
leaving. Alone.

One of the biggest mistakes I see in meetings, interviews, nego-
tiations, pickups: people who aren't smart enough to leave when the
going's good. If you want to make an impression, leave them wanting more.

Break It Down

As with any great story, there are three critical points (or Acts) that make up a meeting. Each Act has a distinct purpose and flow. There's a beginning (Get to Know Me), middle (Climax), and end (Get the Hell Out); and the better you understand what you want to put into, and get out of, each scene, the better.

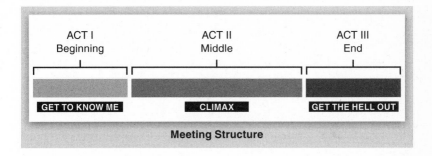

Meeting Structure

Act I—get to know me

The first Act of any meeting is critical. Not only does it set the tone, but the person on the other side of the desk is doing everything in her power to get a handle on you as quickly as possible. She's assessing everything from your posture to how you're wearing your hair. First impressions are lasting so it's right here, in the get-to-know-me phase, where you are making your mark and positioning for the upper hand. There's no reason to go into this first phase without being armed and ready. You should know something about the person and company you're meeting with so you can immediately establish a level of "she's just like me" tribalism. Here's your meeting entrance checklist:

Gloss: Right before you're about to arrive, reapply a little lip gloss . . . a confidence boost in a tube.

Technology: Cell phone, iPod, BlackBerry, whatever your device du jour, switch it off or to silent (no vibrate—it's just as noisy and even more awkward when it rings).

Hair: Make sure your mane's pulled back and out of your face so you won't have to keep wiping at it while you're trying to get down to business.

Handshake: People are more likely to overlook visible piercings than an ineffective handshake, according to a survey of human resources professionals. Pat your slimy palms dry before you go in (try running them under a hand dryer after using a towelette—works like a charm) and offer a sturdy, two-pump grip.

Taking a seat: If you're not the one hosting the meeting, wait to be offered a seat before you start peeling off your outdoor layers and making yourself at home. If you haven't been offered a place to hang your coat, lay it neatly over the back of your chair. If you don't know going into the meeting who's the decision maker, he'll usually enter the room last and have a seat at the head of the table.

Bags: This isn't your bedroom. It's not even your office. So don't go scattering your belongings all over the place. Take out anything you might use in the meeting (pen, notepad, portfolio) and keep it in your lap so you don't have to go digging for it when the time is right. Keep your bag or briefcase zippered and tucked neatly under or beside your chair so no one trips and breaks a nose. (This actually happened to a friend during a dinner meeting—take no chances.)

Small talk: It's fine to make a comment on the weather or compliment their office décor, but you should really follow their lead when it comes to setting the pace. If they're ready to get down and dirty, don't distract them with sweet nothings.

Trick of the Trade: Be Occasionally Unavailable

It's as simple as this: available = easy, easy = undesirable. Successful, talented, in-demand people have schedules that are booked weeks in advance. While I'm not going to suggest a hard-and-fast, "Don't accept a Friday meeting after Tuesday" rule, there's nothing wrong with and everything right about having a schedule that creates an air of mystery and demand.

Act II—climax

Now that you're past the niceties, it's time to get down to business. The biggest mistake you can make during the climax is not to have a crystal-clear agenda and intention for the meeting. What do you want? Whether it's to leave with his number or sell your prototype, know what you're in for. Please, please, please: Keep Your Mouth Shut to ensure you don't give way too much away, and use questions to control the pace and direction of the conversation. The best climaxes are had together, so the name of the game is to find a place where you're both satisfied. You know they're ready to reach their peak when they start using the term "we" in the future tense. To get yours, negotiate your peak:

Get your emotions under control. Though the discussion may get heated, remain calm, don't interrupt (or allow yourself to be interrupted) and listen carefully to get a handle on the other party's point of view.

Find the "why" spot. Why are they refusing to bend *here* while conceding *there*? Dig for the answers that will allow you to propose trade-offs. For example, if you're trying to negotiate a raise and the answer's "no" because they can't incur the extra taxes, you could ask for transportation reimbursement, extra vacation days, or increased expense allowances.

Explore the possibilities. Together, come up with as many potential solutions as you can. Describe what's in it for him each time you propose an idea, and stress that you don't want to leave him high and dry. Once you have him buttered up, you can narrow down your options to win-win.

Act III—get the hell out

This is where all your hard work can go down the drain in an instant. After somewhere between thirty and fifty minutes, the euphoria rubs off and both you and your pitch start to lose your luster. The illusion is always better than the reality, and if you feed her too much at your first sitting, she's going to be full before you get your end of the deal. Give her too much time and her logical brain will leap into action and she'll seek out the holes and start to rationalize how and why this won't work. Just like you need to leave the party at its peak, you need to get out just before it feels like it's time. If you're going to err on one side or the other, go early . . . and leave her wanting more.

It's always in hindsight when I think to myself, "I should have bailed earlier." It can be surprisingly tough to get out when you're excited, you've built momentum, and you just can't stop yourself from going on . . . and on . . . and on. I've trained myself to watch for three very specific signs. See these and get on your way.

The boss stands up. Here's an easy rule: When he stands up, you stand up. And when you stand up, you leave. Simple as that. It doesn't matter if you're in the middle of a statement or defusing a nuclear warhead. You leave.

Fiddling. I don't care if fiddling raises its ugly head in the form of spinning a pencil, jingling change, picking nails—it's a sign that he's losing interest. So wrap it up.

Checking e-mail. Checking e-mail, checking voice mail, surfing porn—you get the picture. You've lost his attention. And it doesn't matter if you're spouting the secret to eternal youth or a dozen Hail Marys, he's not listening, no matter how many times he nods and says, "Uh-huh."

In the Neighborhood

This trick isn't for everyone, but if you're anything like me, you're way better in person than on the phone or on paper. So you need to do everything in your power to get face to face. Whenever I want a meeting, I just happen to be in the 'hood. It's an amazing way to score a lucky-for-him opportunity to meet you while you're in town for other business. I've called everyone from the Dean of Admissions at Cambridge, England, to let him know I was arriving to tour the campus to having my agent schedule my first round of meetings with publishers around my imaginary trip to New York City from Vancouver. Busy people are hard to pin down and an imposed timeframe around your flight can get the meeting on the books. The key is to (a) give them enough advance notice, (b) offer up at least three days of options, and (c) don't book your flight until you get confirmation (it's not 100 percent foolproof and I don't want you calling me looking for your flight to be reimbursed).

Huge disclaimer: Do *not* just land on their doorstep. That's inappropriate, desperate, and will just put them off. Call them in advance and have an actual appointment.

Encore!

So how, after leaving him with desire in his heart, do you ensure a follow-up performance? Three things:

Leave him something to remember you by. People remember very little of what you actually say: it's your energy, enthusiasm, and positivity that stick. Leave him a delighted smile and confident handshake . . . and a business card to make it easy to find you.

Send word. Unlike the arena of dating, do not wait the requisite three days to drop a note of thanks or follow-up e-mail (if you must). I'm a big believer in the power of a handwritten note. Buy yourself some personalized stationary, and literally, the minute you land back to your house or the office, get out a pen and actually write down "great to meet you." A physical note has more impact than an e-mail because it feels more personal and, frankly, way too few people are doing it. But the real trick is to get it in the mail no later than the next day. The goal of the note is to keep the momentum going. This doesn't need to be a tome: like the meeting, keep it brief.

Back on the radar. You don't want to be a stalker, but if a few weeks go by and you haven't heard from her, there's no harm in contacting her again. If you talked about her love of Lebanese food in your meeting, send her a link to a new restaurant in her neighborhood. Just enough effort to put you back on her radar.

Chapter 15

Keep the Fire Alive

There's a monumental difference between want and need. A want you can live without; a need, you can't (or so it feels). We've already been through this—we're all dispensable, but the key to provoking and maintaining the feeling of need is all about igniting a big, hot, fast fire . . . and then keeping it alive. A critical part of your job both in the initial courting and the longer-term committed stage of your professional "relationship" is to maintain the heat. Other prettier, smarter options are always going to be vying for your position—be the keeper.

Sparking the Fire

What is the spark exactly? Perhaps what's more pressing is what the spark is *not*. Nope, it's not knowing he's got hemorrhoids or asking him to pick up tampons. The spark is chemistry, and chemistry can't happen when there's nothing left to the imagination.

The occurrence of a chemical reaction depends on what both parties bring to the table, and while you can't predict what kind of mood he'll be in or what precisely he's looking for, there are a couple of moves you can pull to entice your target to take the bait. All business relationships need to start somewhere, and whether it's at a networking event, on a flight, or in an interview, your job is to captivate your audience.

Looking for a boy's-eye view, I corralled all the men in the office and asked them to reveal what works when it comes to igniting a spark. Here's the fantasy scene they laid out for me, and then my take on the situation. Turns out that even though the lessons originated in a bar, they apply just as thoroughly when establishing relationships in the business world. We're talking first encounter here. This is before you landed the job, the date, the contract. First impressions count, and the more intense the spark, the hotter the flame will grow.

You make eye contact

He says: You've spotted me from across the bar and you wait until I look your way to begin working your voodoo magic (yep, an expression one of the guys used). When your eyes lock with mine, you curl up the corners of your lips, and give a slight raise of an eyebrow.

I say: You'd be surprised how many people don't get the balance between stalker stare and confident contact. Your ability to actually look me in the eyes is a biggie in establishing trust and proving you're not a pushover. They say the eyes are the window to the soul, and if you're hiding yours, you're not getting past go.

You look good

He says: You're made up, but not too made up, and you're dressed in something that makes me think you might be just a tad out of my league. I don't care what brand of jeans you're wearing, just that they're tight (and why exactly are we paying two hundred bucks?).

I say: I don't know you. And that means that I'm using everything in my power to pin you down and the fact that you didn't bother to brush your hair or polish your shoes tells me there's no need to take this any further. This is your first impression and I don't want to see what downhill from here looks like.

You don't say too much

He says: You don't tell me the long and tired story of how you ended up in this town, how you're drinking away your sorrows, and how, lucky for me, you're newly single since your boyfriend broke up with you last night. You offer only snippets from the highlight reel to whet my appetite, hinting that the sum is greater than its parts . . . and if I'm lucky enough, I just might get to see it.

I say: If by the end of the conversation I know that your mother's going through menopause or that you go to see a therapist once a week, it's Game Over. Nothing squelches chemistry like neurosis. I have a sneaking suspicion you're going to be more work than you're worth.

You play coy

He says: You let me search for a sign that the attraction is mutual, but you certainly don't come right out and say it. As much as I don't want to know your entire life story, I also don't want to know you're interested . . . yet. So let me poke around like Curious George while I have fun figuring it out for myself.

I say: I'm a smart girl. You don't need to tell me you're the bomb; I'll figure it out. There is this fine line between a healthy dose of confidence and in-your-face egotism, and if you say that my company or I can't live without you, my first reaction is going to be, "Oh yeah?"

You have to be somewhere else

He says: Tell me you're glad we've met and looking forward to the next time and let me know you need to get on your way. Take my number, offer one last irresistible smile, a lingering handshake, and then let me watch you walk away.

I say: The fact that you have somewhere to go and someone to meet (as long as we're not fifteen minutes into the interview) isn't a bad thing. In fact, if you're in demand, it only makes me want you more.

You're casual on the follow-up

He says: When you shoot me an e-mail the next day, or (preferably) three days later, don't send a novel about why you think
we'd be great together, that you miss me, and that you're counting the minutes until we meet again. And don't send me an
e-mail every day henceforth until I write back. Too much
follow-up equals way too much baggage. Instead, keep it short
and sweet, leaving me to contemplate all the questions I might
ask you on the first date.

I say: If there are four e-mails waiting in my in box when I return,
I'll start to second-guess your mental stability. Sure, you can
be persistent, but give me room to deal with first things first,
or all I'll know is that you're an investment that will never pay
off, given the exhausting amount of attention you require.

Stoking the Fire

Okay, so once you've sparked his interest and he's digging you in
the form of a long-term commitment, now your job is to keep the
fire alive. I'm into year three of my relationship with my business
partner/investor, and not only are the complacency and comfort that
come with time an issue, it's also the fact that he has a wee case of
attention deficit disorder. As with most brilliant, extremely successful, and in-demand people, vying for and capturing his attention for
more than five minutes demands the work of a master.

First and foremost, you need to be unpredictable. Mix it up. If he always knows what position you're going to take, he'll stop asking for your opinion and input. Your boss is constantly being slammed with new, eager talent. Just because you've landed the prize doesn't mean you can sit back and enjoy the ride. Keep up on industry trends or other fresh meat will be replacing you in a heartbeat.

And speaking of keeping it fresh, I've come to understand what I've heard guys complaining about for years. I get that imitation is the sincerest form of flattery, but it's kinda creepy that six months into our relationship you dress, talk, and twirl your hair just like me. Your boss doesn't want a clone or a yes-girl. Keeping the fire alive is all about the spark, and sparks don't fly when you agree with anything and everything he has to say. While there are some exceptions, the majority of successful people surround themselves with minions who'll challenge, disagree, and have the courage enough to say "no."

And finally, this one is critical. Between a boss with both a short attention span and an insatiable need to be fed deliverables regularly, stoking the fire is all about your ability to master the art of putting out exactly and *only* when you need to. If you give him too much at once, not only will he begin to expect that level of output on a regular basis, but he won't appreciate it. Save up some "I've got great news" successes to get you through the dry patches.

Trick of the Trade: Fire with Fire

Someone has an eye on your prize? Wants your man, your job, your promotion? The only way to fight fire . . . is with fire. While this doesn't mean you have to stoop to her nasty, back-stabbing level (but feel free if that's what it takes), it *does* mean that you need to make it crystal clear that you are standing your ground and ready to fight for what's yours.

Extinguishing the Fire

There's a point when either you (or he) will want to put this fire out. Walking away from a professional relationship without proper dousing can have long-lasting career impact. You've invested a lot of time and energy here and it can all go up in smoke.

Tell them yourself

While you wish you could text him to let him know not to expect you back today, tomorrow, *ever,* you can't. You're a big girl and need to face the hard conversation. Quitting can be emotional, both for you and for him, so preplan (even rehearse) what you want to lay down. And then expect he's going to ask you two things:

1. Why aren't you happy?

Feel free to fib a little here—better he doesn't know you think he's a moron. If you're smart, you're actually going to turn this into a compliment. "You inspired me to want to try on a new position." "You taught me more than I ever could have imagined and now I feel like it's time to spread my wings." The safest way to get out of this one is the ole *It's not you, it's me* routine.

2. What can I do to make you stay?

By the time you're quitting, you really should be ready to walk out the door. Promises that he'll change and offers of more money or responsibility, while flattering and tempting, don't usually mean much. When it's done, it's done, and even if you do take him back, he won't have his heart in it, expecting you're on your way out the door.

If you're the one getting doused, whatever you do, don't leave his office without asking why. Whatever he says, amp it up at least 10 percent. Unless it's a bitter breakup, he won't tell you just how bad you were any more than you want to hear it. And no matter how tempting, don't call him any names. You also want to:

Have a replacement

If you don't want him, it doesn't mean you want someone else to have him, but in the case of your career, you really do. It's going to be infinitely easier on you (way fewer calls asking where the client file, stapler, cafeteria is) if he's already enamored with someone else.

Tie up loose ends

Your departure is the last thing he's going to remember about you so make sure it's good. Assign all unfinished projects to your coworkers and leave your desk looking as spotless as it did on your first day. While you may never want to see or hear from him again, the world is small and you want to be able to show your face around town. Conjure up a dignified departure and you'll leave him thinking he just lost.

Chapter 16

Don't Tell Him You Want a Kid on the First Date

Two words for you: Career Suicide. The image of you in your svelte power suit wheeling and dealing suddenly morphs into frumpy muumuus and visions of you cutting out of important meetings to pick up the kid from ballet class.

This is as politically incorrect but as truthful as I can be: Your impending pregnancy is not music to your employer's ears. Until men can perpetuate the human race, we girls have a very special job to perform and this childbearing thing inevitably impacts how we play our career hand.

Have kids, don't have kids—your choice. Just give him a little time to get to know you before you unload the good news on him.

What About Me?

At least when you're sharing the news with your beau, he's got DNA in the game. Your employer, however, isn't seeing much upside. Your boss's basic fears aren't far off from your baby-daddy's.

You'll be a royal bitch

He knows better than to challenge, criticize, oppose you during that certain time of the month, but nine long months of PMS? He's terrified that his happy little worker bee is going to turn into an unbearable beast. Tears, hissy-fits, no-work standoffs are the all-too-vivid visions running through his head.

The truth of the matter is you *will* be on the emotional edge, and this means you need to rally yourself a support team you can call when you find yourself on the verge of bawling or ripping someone's head off. Your boss doesn't deserve—and won't tolerate—being your whipping boy.

Your performance will decrease

Well, there goes the deed. His basic fear is that all that baby-making business in your body is going to seep the brains out of your head and into your belly. He's scared your much-needed afternoon nap is going to cut into his work time and he's no longer going to see any action.

When haven't women had to do twice the work men do to be considered equally talented? Of course you're happy to do it, but don't hesitate to accept help.

You'll be preoccupied

His primary concern? That he's no longer going to be your number one. He's worried he's going to get lost in the shuffle and lose his place in the pecking order. Who cares about the latest status report when you have a baby brewing?

If ever you've needed to put in face time, it's now. Make sure you're present and, more important, engaged. Ask questions, take initiative, stroke his ego—whatever it takes to ensure he doesn't feel passed over and forgotten.

Trick of the Trade: Watch Your Back

And you thought it was tough to tell your man-boss that you've got a bun in the oven. Just wait until you deliver the good news to all the girls in the office. It's always surprising considering we're from the same tribe, but women can be way harder than most men. Whatever you do, if you're coming back, let it be known. If your coworkers suspect you're "retiring," they'll be vying for your office before you've had your first contraction. And though you may feel like ass warmed over, especially in the beginning months of your pregnancy, don't discuss it—or worse, let them see you napping in your office. While some of your coworkers may sympathize (especially the ones who have kids), others will use your lack of energy as a way to push you off important projects.

No Perfect Time

I've worked with, am friends with, and have been surrounded by women who have played the game in one of two ways: precareer or postcareer. When it comes down to it, there's no perfect time to have a baby, but there are some pros and cons to consider:

Precareer

Pros

- You're fertile and time is on your side. You look and feel fantastic. There's no reason to think you won't be able to get pregnant first go round—and with the sperm donor (um, man) of your choice.
- Your career is always going to be waiting for you, your eggs— not so much. If you're smart (or if you aren't, but can bullshit with the best of them), you'll be able to jump back into the job market with no problem. That baby brain fogginess is reversible, but once your eggs wither up and die, it's over.
- You're not ass-tired and you have enough energy to do it all. You're a superwoman right now—run five miles, work fourteen hours, plan your best friend's bridal shower, meet your new man for drinks—and that's just on Monday. Now picture doing all of that, plus caring for a kid. And oh yeah, you're forty-five.

Cons

- You haven't had enough time to build a reputation and it can be harder to get back in the game. You think you're a star, but no one else has gotten that memo. If you leave now, you'll have to start at square one later—and you'll have to cozy up to your intern, who's now the boss.

- You're in the trenches and not yet in a position of "Can you do this for me?" You haven't earned the right to delegate what you don't want to do to your underlings. Translation: You'll be writing up that weekly report at 8 p.m. on a Friday, and then have to go home and deal with dirty diapers and dinner (which you'll most likely be making).

- You can't afford the massage, the babysitter, the Prozac—to get you through the day. Kids cost a lot of money. It's much easier to buy the $400 shoes when you're the one giving up dinner for a week to pay for them. When it's your kid going hungry? There's a word for that: child abuse.

- You resent not having lived your career dreams . . . yet. If you become a mom before you've become a [insert title here], you're always going to feel resentful—no matter how much you love little Joey. On the trying days—the ones where your kid won't eat, sleep, or shit without crying your name—you'll fantasize about where you'd be if only you had kept working. (Taking your boss's crap is a nonissue. This is a fantasy after all.)

Postcareer

Pros

- You have enough success to weather a lasting departure. You want a six-month maternity leave and a three-day workweek once you come back? If you've racked up some serious money for your firm, you'll probably get it.

- You can afford an army of nannies. Don't be a hero. If you can pay for the help (and you can), hire it.
- You're in a management position and most of your demands can be executed from the comfort of your bed. Ever notice how no one questions the fact that the CEO gets carte blanche to go to every soccer game, ballet recital, or teacher conference she wants? When you're the boss, you choose how and when you work.
- You're flying to Malawi to pick up a kid. When you've achieved Madonna's level of world dominance, there's no wrong time to have a kid—especially when someone else is pushing it out for you.

Cons

- You're sitting pretty in the CEO position and decide you want a child, but your eggs are as old as you feel. Again, you're forty-five. After getting eight hours, it can be hard to pull it together, never mind being up every two to breastfeed. And no matter how in shape you are, your body just isn't going to bounce back the way it would have when you were twenty.
- You spend five years and fifty thousand dollars getting knocked up. It's that whole withering eggs thing. That bun can definitely be put in the oven, but it's going to cost you.
- You simply can't get pregnant. Regret is a bitter pill to swallow. Much more so than the resentment you would have felt if you'd had a kid ten years earlier instead of taking that promotion.
- You're flying to Malawi to pick up a kid. There's something to be said for the act of giving birth. If you wait too long, the choice will be made for you.

Cat's Out of the Bag

The last thing you need is for your office competitor to deliver the good (for her anyway) news. The child's father can come first but second stop is your boss. For one thing, you want to allay all the fears we talked about earlier, and for two, your approach and energy in sharing the news set the tone for the rest of your pregnancy. I know it's only the most significant, life-altering moment of your life, but . . . go light and breezy. I've been preparing to utter the words "I'm pregnant" for, oh, about ten years now and have been closely watching and learning the following tricks to setting yourself up to share the news without being pushed aside.

Leverage a big delivery

So I'm about to break my cardinal rule of telling my significant other (my investor, in my case) the big news but here you have it: I'm going to start trying to get pregnant right around the time this book hits the shelves (say a prayer it's a done deal by the time you're reading these words). The best time to make your announcement is right after producing a significant professional accomplishment that has some legs and will buy you some "Can't live without me" leverage.

Be aware that timing is everything

We pretty much know what pregnancy looks like (ebb and flow of emotion, energy, skin glow) and how long it takes—important information to work with. And while you can't count on the stock market crash or your doctor putting you on bed rest, you do know your business deadlines and cycles (summer hiatus, tax season, fall fashion shows). Some times really are better than others, and birth control was invented for a reason.

Have a drop dead date

You may need to consider your delivery in the context of finding the right guy, a major dream career accomplishment, or both. But I've met enough profoundly disappointed women who have just waited and waited and are now so filled with regret that they didn't pick a date and do it on their own, that it makes me think we all need to have an internal "Enough is enough, this is my drop dead date" in our heads. And then say a prayer that God's willing.

Go it on your own

I'm sure it looks like the reverse is true, but the biggest motivation I have for working my ass off in my business is actually for my child. I knew very early on that I wanted to be able to afford (on all levels) to give my kids the same kind of dedication I had given to my career. This may very well be the biggest gamble of my life but the ultimate leverage is to have your name on the door . . . but not a new door. Give yourself a couple (as in three to five) years to get some momentum and create some success, knowing you will be working 24/7 and that's before the babe arrives.

Back in the Game

I've read a crazy number of stats but here's the gist. While I've met the girl who's on her BlackBerry while she's got her legs up in the delivery room, the majority of women who think they'll go back to work after having a child . . . don't—at least not for three to five years. This is the primary concern and uncertainty of your employer, your clients, your staff—and apparently we're not sure if we're going back either. The best advice I have for you here is to be fair and honest. Address it up front . . . address it along the way . . . address it during the leave . . . address it on your way back . . .

Getting back in the game is a whole book unto itself (and I may very well write it if my eggs cooperate and I've got some experience to go on), but the bottom line message is threefold:

First, if you want to (or have to) go back to work, you can. Keep your résumé updated (fill in the gaps with the skills you've learned while volunteering or corralling herds of toddlers to beginner's ballet). Stay in touch with both industry trends and your peeps (meet with them in person and without the kids tagging along when possible), attend events when you can, and in the end you'll be good to go.

Second, the majority of women who do come back have a whole new set of standards and the name of the game becomes less about quantity and more about quality—which if positioned correctly is very attractive to employers. Consider all your options (working part-time, taking an extra year off, telecommuting, etc.), then go ahead and ask for your ideal schedule. With the push to create mom-friendly work atmospheres, employers are more flexible than ever as long as you demonstrate you can and will produce. Also, it's important to reassess your values—after a life-altering event like having children, you may be looking for more meaningful ways to spend your time away from home.

Last but not least, have faith. I believe with everything in me we can experience both a fulfilling career and a family life (we just need to be realistic and easy on ourselves when we can't do both to perfection at the same time). I meet incredibly driven, success-ful, nurturing, beautiful women who are amazing mothers and awe-inspiring professionals each and every day.

Chapter 17

A Room of One's Own

Not sure how Virginia Woolf would have felt about her call for women's independence to be included in a dating-rule-turned-career book, but who doesn't have an image of herself sitting behind a beautiful desk in a corner office?

Seriously, long before I could have ever known what I was going to do with my career, I knew it would be in a bustling city, in some kind of tall, glass building that would contain my glamorous corner office, communicating some balance between being an extension of my home (the image always contained a couch and some kind of slick coffee table) and signifying that I have arrived.

I honestly believe that the reality of our workspace (and the city we decide to live in) is a reflection of our personalities and influences our output enough to warrant a chapter. We all need a room of one's own—what does yours say about you?

Accoutrements

A friend just invited me on an apartment swap in Paris and I was surprised at (a) just how nosy I am and (b) what a few books and pictures (and psychotropic drugs) can say about you and your life. Beyond the fact that we log more hours in our office than we do our homes, our office communicates way more about us than we care to imagine. Before you're in a position to call the architect and designer to create your own beautiful office, there are simple things that you can do to improve your assigned space and help people get the right impression.

Books

Hello . . . take heed in the whole "You are what you read" school of thought. The books you just happen to have lying around the office are an expression of you, and the Danielle Steele poking out from under your mountain of work is not what you're going for. Here are what some classics are saying about you:

> **A dictionary:** Curious, a stickler for detail, and perhaps a little bit old-school—you're well aware that a seasoned vocabulary is never out of style.

> **Biography:** Whether it's the story of Einstein or Coco Chanel, you're interested in learning from the successes of the best in class.

> ***Good to Great:*** Ambitious, disciplined, willing to improve . . . you were born a leader and won't quit 'til you're at the top.

The 7 Habits of Highly Effective People: Okay, so maybe you've already got this one on the shelf, considering everyone and their moms have received it as a gift at some point. But have you actually read your copy? If you can't actually name the seven habits, start earmarking.

The Tipping Point: You're curious, clued in, and able to recognize a good thing when you see it. Your ability to anticipate trends makes *you* the one in demand.

The One Minute Manager: You've got lots of important matters to tend to, which is why it's so great that you're organized, resourceful, and not out to waste anyone's time—especially your own.

How to Win Friends & Influence People: Ruthless and desperate, maybe, but you can successfully maneuver even the trickiest of conversations—and that makes you one powerful partner.

Pictures

I remember walking into this guy's apartment and thinking, "How sweet, he's got a lot of pictures of his friends and family around." Upon closer inspection, he was in each and every shot. Feel free to bring some pictures to the office, but try not to communicate egomania by being in every one. Also, watch the drunken shots: none of you and the girls knocking back tequila shooters. Pick pictures that show you have an interesting and cultured life (you and your significant other at an Italian vineyard) and that will stimulate conversation.

Flowers

It's going to look a little weird having the big bouquet that stinks of lillies in your cubicle, but a small arrangement of seasonal flowers not only boosts your mood and creativity, but will also help you to forget you've just clocked your fifteenth hour for today and haven't seen nature in three weeks.

Feng Shui Your Way to Success

I loved *Domino* magazine, and flipping through a copy, I happened upon Catherine Brophy, THE feng shui DETECTIVE, and had three inspired thoughts: (1) Who isn't willing to try out a little feng shui? (2) We should really include it in the chapter on space, and (3) Catherine should write it. Thanks, Catherine!

Good feng shui removes barriers to your advancement and lets you shine. Here are Catherine's pointers to help you rise to the top:

- Keep your workspace clean and clear. A clutter-free desk and office not only allow you to function at peak efficiency, but also encourage creativity, along with Chi (energy), to flow. Keep in mind your space reflects who you are. Make sure you are projecting a confident and capable image. If your office is in disarray, that is how people will view you. Get into the habit of cleaning your desk each day before you leave, and generating a task list for the next day. When you come in each morning, you will begin your day with order, focus, and ease.

- If you have control over the placement of your desk, try to sit with your back to a solid wall in the Power Point of the room. The Power Point is the farthest corner diagonally opposite the entry. Sitting in this position will optimize your vantage point. It will activate visibility, so you can both see what's happening around you, and be seen and recognized by others. If you sit with your back to a window, keep the shades down. If your back is exposed to open space and you cannot see behind you, place reflective accessories on your desk. A chrome task lamp, clock, or picture frame placed in front of you will allow you to "watch your back." This will help you feel secure.

- Create a welcoming and inviting space. Make sure nothing blocks the entry and that everything is in good working order. Replace broken clocks, lamps, pens, etc. You and others should feel comfortable in the space. If you can, hang or prop a beautiful piece of art that draws the eye in. You get feng shui bonus points if it relates to your career as well. For example, if you are in publishing, place framed award-winning magazine covers that inspire and excite you where you and others can see them. If you are excited and happy, and everything works well in your space, you will perform better on the job.

A City of One's Own

I can remember it clear as day. I was sitting at Rockefeller Center on the rink-turned-summer restaurant, devouring a plate of French toast, slightly distracted by the spray from the Prometheus fountain, when suddenly I was struck with a premonition. I pulled out a pen and a piece of paper and wrote down:

I am moving to New York City.

At the time this couldn't have been farther from reality. I was married, living in Vancouver, Canada, and while I did have an agent, without a Visa or a real job I would be living on the streets. Over the course of the next three years, inch by inch my life was pulled to the city that both exhilarated and terrified me. I had always heard that you either love or hate New York, but on any given day I was firmly planted on one side or the other. I had a hard time transitioning from tourist to resident, but one day, not long ago, I caught myself crossing Park Avenue, looking down to the MetLife building, and knew that more than a pit stop, this city had become my own. Here's what I learned about moving in.

Make a trip

If you're going to make a move, you can try it on for size in bite-sized increments. For a full year before I actually changed my address, I would come to the city to get a lay of the land. Especially if it's a big move (another country or much larger city). Total immersion on day one can get you back on the plane faster than a roach-infested hotel room. Plan weekend excursions or a week-long trip to get your bearings.

Find some friends

I'm far from a wallflower, so I was shocked to learn how hard it was to make new friends. With visions of *Sex and the City* dancing through my head, I kept looking for Charlotte and Miranda. I'd meet interesting women but they'd be (a) too old (boring), (b) too young (infantile), (c) married (attached at the hip), (d) raising kids (the noise), (e) not like my best friends at home (but who is?), or (e) attached to my work (I was paying them or they were paying me). I'm all about having the right work-based friendships, but honestly, it wasn't until I started to make friends with people outside the office and got over the fact that I didn't need replacements for the old ones that I started to find new friends and began to feel like I belonged. Whatever it is that you enjoy doing (running, knitting, reading), join a club that will introduce you to new and interesting people . . . and be open-minded. Those oldies can be goodies.

Settle in

In the first two months I lived in New York, I was at the Metropolitan Museum of Art once (sometimes twice) a week. In the last two years, I haven't made it there at all. The amazing thing about moving to a new place is the opportunity to live in a city as a tourist, but at a certain point, it's important (or it was for me at least) to actually move in and build a neighborhood of local haunts and get to know the regulars. You know you belong when you find coffee that isn't Starbucks and they know what you want before you ask for it.

Become a new you

So remember the trip to Paris I told you about? Surrounded by the most spectacular-looking women and stores galore, I went on a little spree and ended up sporting some getups I wouldn't be caught dead in at home but felt amazing in on the streets of Paris. The worst and best part of being in a new city is that no one knows you. You can be anyone and anything you want to be. You get to throw off the old (dysfunctional friendships, misperceptions of yourself, good-girl reputation) and you get to try on the new you.

Where the Jobs Are

You're about as likely to land the job of your dreams living in Podunk, Kentucky (Population: 93), as you are to meet the man of your dreams. (You've gotta go where the numbers are.) If you want the high-powered job, you have to make the move to a high-powered location, where connections that matter can be made the moment you step out your front door.

New York. Teeming with young professionals, and well, people of any kind really, this is where you want to be for all things fashion, finance, or publishing related. New York City is home to financial monster JPMorgan Chase and media conglomerate News Corp., not to mention the nonstop nightlife and world-class dining.

San Francisco. Where culturally rich meets high-tech, San Francisco is a hotbed for innovation and creativity. Silicon Valley hosts a large number of engineers, venture capitalists, and tech businesses including the "it" firm Google—not to mention some of the fittest residents in the United States (bring your flats—you'll be walking everywhere!).

Chicago. You may need to hit up the Magnificent Mile for gloves and scarves when you get here. The Windy City lies on the tip of Lake Michigan and the wind chill falls below zero regularly during the winter—a small price to pay for the chance to work for big players like DDB Advertising, Allstate, or oh yeah, Oprah. And if you like hot dogs and sports, you'll be two steps ahead in the dating game!

Los Angeles. If you want anything to do with motion pictures, television, or music, head to L.A. and don't look back. 20th Century Fox, Warner Bros., and Columbia Pictures are just a few of the big-wig entertainment leaders in the City of Angels. But you've got to look the part if you want to get anywhere here—stop on Rodeo Drive for the must-have bag and sunglasses of the season (a boob job probably wouldn't hurt, either) before "networking" at Chateau Marmont.

Washington, D.C. If you want to build an impressive résumé, the nation's capital can help. Whether your goal is to be a Congressional aide on Capitol Hill or to conduct research at any of the nearby universities, one thing's for sure—you won't dumb it down in D.C.! With the abundant museums and historic sites, you'll be able to catch up on everything you missed in Econ.

Boston. This colonial town is brimming with young researchers, biotechnologists, and number crunchers working at companies like EMC, Merck & Co., and Fidelity Investments. You'll score points if you're Irish and can nail down the Boston accent—and while you're at it, catch yourself a Harvard grad!

Seattle. Get your foot in the door at Starbucks before it takes over the entire world, or join any of the other well-established companies such as Amazon, Adobe Systems, or Nordstrom. Sure, it may be rainy most of the time, but you'll be too busy enjoying your time meeting friends for coffee or checking out the killer alternative music scene to notice.

Minneapolis. Though it might not *sound* exciting, Minneapolis is actually home of some of the most reputable corporations in America, including Target, Best Buy, IBM, Wells Fargo, and ING Group. If you're looking to climb the corporate ladder, get your start in the Twin Cities.

Chapter 18
Watch Your Weight

A nd you thought a hot guy was the key to keeping your ass in shape. What if I told you that watching your weight would mean career success? More passion, prestige, power, money—it all could be yours. Now that's worth getting off the couch.

Again, this may send me to feminist hell, but I truly believe that your weight, and even more than that, your level of physical fitness, has a much-bigger-than-you'd-think impact on your career. Not only because of how other people perceive you (worst case: lazy) and how you feel about yourself (best case: powerful), but also because of its sheer influence on your level of performance. Time and time again I've tested the power of making the connection between a physical and a career goal and I've found that raising your pulse is a quick and easy trick to increase your level of endurance, your ability to take risk, and your willingness to do what's hard.

Make a Run for It

Five years ago the only thing I was more afraid of than writing a book was hitting the streets in a pair of running shorts. That all turned around the day I watched my insane triathlete friend clock more miles of physical activity than I would ever even consider driving. As she crossed the finish line cloaked with a level of energy, inspiration, and motivation that was palpable, all I could think was . . . I need to get me some of that.

The next day, in the face of plotting out an actual pen-to-page schedule for bringing my imaginary book to life, I decided I would run my way to completion. To this day, I honestly believe with everything in me that running was the one and only way I got my first bitch of a book done and here's why:

Put a time on it

So the first day I set out without a watch. I ran for as far as my little legs would take me, came home, and told anyone who would listen that I had run for twenty minutes. The next day I tried again. Going past my initial marker, I hit twenty-five minutes. The third time I set out, I took the watch my beau had bought me to celebrate my newfound fitness, hit my mark, and was devastated to learn that, yeah, I had just run seven fucking minutes. Fitness is all about numbers—minutes, miles, repetition—the quantification of progress, exertion, and delivery. People tend to underestimate both the amount of actual time it takes to succeed and the time they spend in the pursuit of their goal—it may feel like a lot but it ain't. Translate your seven-minute run into thirty minutes on your new business proposal. Time yourself. Success does not come without quantifiable effort.

Drug of choice

Whenever I have a career-related task that I am truly and utterly afraid of, I take it on immediately (not hours, not days, but minutes) after I've increased my heart rate. Every day after my run, without changing my stinky sweaty clothes, I'd sit down at the computer and write. Endorphins are as good as cocaine (or so I'm told) in making you believe you're the queen of the world and able to accomplish anything—use them.

Go Zen

I'm not going to lie to you, my first few runs I was like, "This is batshit boring." It was pre-iPods, and even though I was in the spectacular city of Vancouver, it was near impossible to get my brain to rest. *What am I going to eat when I'm done? I'm tired; I should really call my mom* . . . But once I actually hit the thirty-minute mark, something marvelous began to happen . . . peace. It's different for everyone but there's an immersion marker where you slip into a meditative, out-of-your-head state that is your creative wellspring. Start a workout with a question, problem, or issue that you're not sure how to solve and by the end you'll have, if not the answer, an infinitely clearer perspective.

Feel the pain

I remember watching an interview with Lance Armstrong and he essentially said that his cancer and treatments prepared him to be a champion. That his experience of and tolerance for pain are simply beyond that of his competitors. In America the majority of us live not only free of real pain but we expect things to go our way quickly and easily. Physical exertion is an incredible teacher and the true conduit for success. We all have imaginary limits, but it is an amazing experience to actually *feel* them. I never would have anticipated that building a business, leaving a husband, loving my aging nana would be this hard or painful, but running has taught me that just when you think you can't take one step more . . . you can.

Top Ten Reasons Why Going to the Gym Is Good for Your Career

1. It's a stress reliever that won't get you fired—unlike punching your entitled assistant in the face the next time she tells you she doesn't "do" lunch orders.

2. A strong body breeds a strong mind.

3. You'll have more energy—and might even stay awake during your boss's mind-numbing three-hour meetings.

4. You'll meet people—whether that be a boyfriend or a billionaire willing to invest in your next great idea.

5. Your yoga breaths will come in handy every time your cubicle mate starts telling you about her tantric sex sessions—in detail.

6. You want to join the company softball team. You saw what happened to the last wuss who couldn't keep up.

7. The IT hottie told you he met his ex while working out.

8. A black suit can only hide so much chub.

9. You catch your CEO checking out your biceps appreciatively.

10. If you don't get the promotion, you can always take her down in a dark alley.

Different Stokes for Different Folks

So the best thing about exercise is all the options. I don't care if you're using sex or a Stairmaster, it's about getting your heart rate up and experiencing your physical prowess. Here are some options and what they're good for:

Running

Because running is such a pure exertion of energy, I love to hit the streets when I am pissed off, feel stressed, or need to shake off any kind of negative energy. You can use music to escape your brain (and reality), but I prefer to hear and focus on my breath (which is usually labored).

Spin

I spin first thing in the morning, and nine times out of ten, I start the class tired and already planning to sneak out early. And then . . . the music, sitting behind the girl with the killer ass, the simple instruction and rhythm of the pedals . . . all bring me to this place of pure energy and problem solving. Get on a bike when you have a problem to solve or something to create.

Golf

Golf is a total diversion and a psychological addiction more powerful than most opiates. Eighteen holes is four hours of focus on the ridiculously inane task of getting a little white ball into a hole. And while it won't shave inches off your thighs, there are ancillary benefits: There aren't nearly as many women who play "client golf" as men. If you're one of them, you automatically gain a certain amount of respect from the boys' club. And if you happen to look good in a golf skirt (and have a decent swing), you have a devastating business advantage. Also more career moves are made on the nineteenth hole (the bar at the end of a round) than almost anywhere else I know.

Tennis

Tennis is the Swiss Army Knife of sports. It combines the agility of basketball, the coordination of baseball, the aerobics of running, and the strategy of golf. It can be social (doubles) or solo. If you like developing a skill as you develop your body, this jack-of-all-trades sport is for you.

Swimming

After getting my period at eleven and spouting breasts that even my skin-tight leotard couldn't contain, my dreams of being an Olympic gymnast were dashed. So where does a girl with boobs, flexibility, and an uncanny ability to hold her breath end up? The local swimming pool. The opportunity to sink beneath the surface and escape the world, the relaxing rhythm of the stroke, and the lean legs that come from hanging on to the kickboard make swimming an exercise that relieves the tension in your head without inflicting any stress on your body. Slather your hair in olive oil, put it in a cap, and you'll be conditioned all over.

Pilates

Not only does Pilates help you learn how to breathe (yes, there is a correct way), but every time you do so, you're strengthening your core, which gives you rock-hard abs, better posture, and a longer, leaner appearance. Pilates makes you feel strong on the outside (and the inside), which is exactly what you need when you're about to conquer the career world.

Join Forces

I knew he was the one for me when, just like I'd scurry to pick up all the stuff lying around my apartment before the cleaning lady came over, I found myself working out in between our sessions so that I'd look as he calls it "slammin'." I'm all about hiring yourself a trainer to get yourself in gear and especially one that's hot and talented enough to make you (a) more than willing to do one more set (wouldn't want him to think you're a quitter) and (b) in perfect form (sure to look better with your shoulders back). Even if you can't or won't invest in a trainer, there are a few tricks to the discipline trade:

Have a routine

That triathlete friend of mine I mentioned earlier puts it this way: "I'm tired when I wake up at six and I'm tired when I wake up at seven." It's true. When are you not exhausted rolling out of bed in the morning? The trick of making exercise a part of your life is not to think about it, but as Nike so aptly puts it, just do it. Create a schedule and stick to it. No excuses. Even if you're not a morning person, you're more likely not to bail if you work out in the morning—can't blame the boss for keeping you late.

Lay out your stuff

Okay, so one of the best parts of exercising? You can get yourself a whole new wardrobe! It's a great excuse to go shopping and there are some amazing clothes on the market that straddle the real-world line (just don't wear your yoga pants to the office). Lay out your Stella McCartney for Adidas and Vancouver-born lululemon gear in the morning so you have one less thing to think about.

Mix it up

Variety is the spice of life, and if you want to keep it interesting, you're going to have to switch it up. Not only will it help keep you motivated and engaged (a big part of what keeps you out of your head and coming back for more is the challenge of mastering a new sport) but your body is supersmart, and when you do the same exercise repeatedly, it becomes increasingly efficient, which means you don't burn as many calories as you would trying something new.

Join in

This isn't rocket science. If you've paid a trainer or if you've got a friend waiting at the gym for you to show up, you've got a little extra incentive to get out the door. Ideally exercise will become a habit in your life, but in the meantime, build in some accountability. Whether it be a fear of disappointing a friend, a hot date, or a killer promotion—use what you've got to get your ass in gear.

Chapter 19

Have Others Sing Your Praises

Have you ever seen a mother's face when she's told her kid has talent? A guy whose buddy says his new girlfriend is hot? Complete and total elation. The true art of the game is to build a network of supporters who are on the streets singing your praises to anyone and everyone who'll listen. Even the most secure businesspeople like to have their decisions validated, and I promise there is nothing better than your boss being congratulated for finding a star like you.

Rally the Troops

You need to come to this whole concept from the perspective that, while people really do like to help others, the reality is they're lazy. Make it easy for them to sing your praises and you'll be laughing all the way to career success.

Define the message

The last thing you want is your Aunt Sally telling everybody within range that it's been months since you've worked for money after being let go at your last gig. If you're on the market, you want to arm your troops with the right message. Don't leave Aunt Sally up to her own devices (and interpretation). Let her know your amazingly talented ass is being pursued by a number of big players, and while you're not sure who you're going to go with, you're still welcoming other offers. People not only believe but *repeat* what you tell them. Control your message.

Give them a package

Okay, so if Aunt Sally simply isn't the smartest girl in the world, give her a package of material that does all the work for her. Your résumé, portfolio, media kit—let your presentation do the talking.

Don't make an ass of them

Most important thing of all: If they've gone to the trouble of extending their reputation to recommend you, you better be good. The key to ensuring you're worth bragging about is to follow up with your very best game and deliver beyond anyone's expectations. Be careful not to disappoint.

Be hot

I still remember the person who told me about *DailyCandy* the first month they were in business. Her recommendations are always dead-on and her referral to a newsletter that keeps you in touch with the latest and greatest was no different. The lesson here is twofold: (a) If at all possible, put your message in the hands of the go-to girl (or guy), the person people seek out for keeping them up to date on what's hot, and (b) position yourself as something up-and-coming. Everyone wants to believe they are a trend spotter and ahead of the curve—make sure *you're* the next big thing.

Get on their back

Again, this comes down to the lazy factor (that or they suspect you don't have it and they aren't willing to risk their reputation). If they've promised to spread the word and haven't delivered, you need to find the line between stalker and irritating enough to want to get you out of their hair. Make the call already!

Let them be the matchmaker

If you're still resistant to ask for help, just remember the pride your grandmother takes in having set up Billy with Mary back in 1947. People really do want to do good for others. Consider it a favor.

Make payment

Once they've introduced you to your future employer, talked you up all over town, or offered to edit your résumé, make sure to thank them for their efforts. A handwritten note, flowers, a box of goodies from their favorite bakery—it all makes them feel as though their time was worth it. Plus, it gives them another reason to brag about you.

Pay For the Pleasure

When Aunt Sally just isn't getting the deal done, it may be time to hire the big guns: the publicist and the headhunter. One will spread your name around town, and the other will help you land the job of your dreams.

The publicist

I've been through this enough times to know better, but each and every time I meet a new publicist I feel the excitement of finding a long-lost soul mate of a best friend. She "gets" the business, is willing to work night and day to land me on *Oprah* and have me profiled in *Vogue*. What I tend to forget is that these people are experts at blowing smoke and they're drinking their own Kool-Aid. I've been around this block enough times to help guide your selection:

What to look for

First, whether you're looking to hire a personal publicist or an entire firm to pimp you out, it's essential to find someone with an established relationship with the media. And not just any media— the right media. Whether your wish list includes *BusinessWeek* or *Bon Appétit,* know where you want to be, and make sure they've already got those key players on speed dial. The time they waste meeting and greeting is your money down the drain. And if they whore your brand around for just anyone's taking, you'll watch your credibility go down with it.

Second, look for a proven track record. You're not paying them to learn the game, you're paying them to help you bed a handsome front-page hit—so do your research. Where have their clients been featured before? What do their references have to say? Contacts are what counts—now's not the time to take a chance on an ambitious beginner.

Finally, find someone with a level of aggression that suits you and your business. Your representation will be a direct reflection of you. If she's mastered the art of being firm without acting desperate, she could be a keeper.

How to Find the Right Fit

Unfortunately, you can't truly know how the PR glove fits until you try it on. But there are some steps you can take to hedge your bets. A good place to start is to check out your competitor's press. Note who's been making headlines and find out who's doing their dirty work.

Keep in mind, though, that success on someone else's behalf doesn't automatically translate to success on yours. If a firm doesn't wholeheartedly believe in you and your mission, you won't be their top priority. And if you're just one of many on their roster, you can bet they'll book everyone else on *Today* before they start calling the local paper to see if they might squeeze you in.

When you've obtained a few leads, it's time to start doing some background checking. Get ahold of some of their current clients and ask the bottom-line questions the firm itself will skirt around: How long do you have to wait until your phone is ringing off the hook with people who want what you've got? If you're going to be two-timed, you might as well use the other woman for her valuable insights.

Once you've got a potential fit, make them whet your appetite. They've got to earn your business. Ask for sample campaigns, a proposal, whatever it takes to assure you they'll get the job done. In the process, make sure to meet your account manager—the person on their end who will be largely responsible for either failing miserably or pleasantly surprising you. Beware that many firms place rookie team members on lower-profile accounts, and you want to be treated like the main dish, not the mistress.

When it becomes time to talk money, if at all possible, avoid pay until you get some play. Many firms ask for a set fee up front, which often leads to you writing checks while you're still sitting high and dry. Find one that offers a pay-for-performance fee—or include an opt-out period in the contract. It's also important to make sure both sides are clear on what's expected from the relationship. Is it a one-time fling? Will you be allowed to see other firms? Can they make the commitment to a long-term media marriage? Know what you're after, or you're bound to end up bitter, divorced, and ransacked for all your hard-earned money.

What to Expect

As your relationship with your PR team develops, there are some standards that should be set from the beginning. Reliability, dependability, and constant course correcting are what it's all about.

Expect him to be in touch regularly. You shouldn't be hard pressed to get the guy on the phone—you're his number one priority after all. If he's not up to date on your daily affairs, how will he know whom to go after? And if he's not reporting his progress, how will you know he's doing his job? Another reason to be in constant contact is to fine-tune how you work together so you can achieve maximum results. Review what's worked and what hasn't, and continue to develop new plans of attack.

Not only does he need to be accessible, but he's got to be loyal. Of course, you probably don't plan on ramming umbrellas into car windows or driving with your baby in your lap, but you don't want your publicist to toss you by the wayside like Britney if and when your company is critiqued. At the end of the day, he's got to be willing to stick by your side.

Finally, it's worth mentioning that while having too much patience can leave you broke and abused, a certain amount of trust and understanding is required. Chances are, your publicist won't turn you into an overnight sensation. Expect low-level results in the short-term, and high-level results to follow. Give your team space to do their jobs right and allow time for your brand to grow—the outcome will be worth waiting for.

The headhunter

They seem like the answer to your prayers: the person who will get you out of the hellhole of a job you've been buried in for the last five years. But while headhunters promise a lot on your first meeting, they may not always deliver—or return your calls. And since you usually aren't paying them out of your own pocket (the company that ultimately hires you pays for their services), demanding attention from them can be futile, especially since they've seen ten candidates as qualified as you before they've even taken their mid-morning coffee break.

What to Look For

The key to finding a reputable matchmaker is to ask for referrals. Find friends who've scored some major tail and borrow their resources. Then be sure to investigate success rates. Do a large percentage of the search firm's setups live happily ever after?

It's also important to make sure your search firm has experience with your industry. Just like you'd never join JDate if you're Catholic or eHarmony if you're under forty, you'll never net your dream job if they're fishing in the wrong pond. Headhunters often have a specific demographic they deal with. Make sure they'll be able to accommodate your taste and that they'll be able to provide plenty of options that fit the bill and have an extensive network of companies to reach out to.

How to Find the Right Fit

First of all, it's important to know the difference between "contingency" and "retained" search firms. (Keep in mind that *neither* are working for you—they're working for the employer.) A contingency firm will get paid only if they find the company a suitable mate. They normally work with low- to mid-level professionals, and since they have a set fee per placement, they're usually handling a number of companies (and other clients) at a time. On the other hand, retained firms have been hired on an exclusive basis with a company to find "the one," and they're usually paid a one-time fee of about a third of the salary of the candidates they place. A retained firm will have a limited number of opportunities to offer you, but when they do, these will likely be high-paying positions in large and/or prestigious companies. No matter what, though, you should never agree to pay a firm on the promise that they'll find you work.

Once you've found a cost-effective option, ask what kind of processes they use for identifying candidates. Will personality and skill sets be considered? You're not about to leave one dead-end relationship for another.

Again, background checking is a must. Speak with the firm's past clients for a run-down on your matchmaker and how to get the most from them. If you stay top of mind, will they work harder on your behalf? Do they like to be buttered up? Do they accept bribes? (Kidding, but not really. I've heard of some desperate attempts to get on *Oprah*.) Also make sure to find out who will be doing the actual search. A seasoned expert will ask you the right questions and get a complete picture of what you're looking for, whereas a new hire with no Rolodex might just go by what looks like a match on paper.

To make sure your new headhunter won't be a waste of time and money, provide a list of companies you'd like them to pursue, and be as detailed as possible in your job requirements. The better they know your type, the more compatible the matches are likely to be.

What to Expect

Your search firm will prep you for the first date. They'll give you the 411 on whom you'll be meeting and what role he plays. They should also follow up for the scoop on how it went. (How interested did he seem? Did he give you the tour of his place? Did he introduce you to his friends?) But they won't do all the work, so don't rest on your laurels. When the firm comes back to you with potentials, be ready with the right questions. (Why is he single? Whom does he run with?) Finally, know that true love doesn't happen overnight. Thorough searches can take several months. Be patient and wait for the right one.

Chapter 20

Be Willing to Walk Away

As I'm writing this last chapter and procrastinating my ass off, I know with utter certainty that I have an issue with letting go. It was actually my beloved brother who pointed this one out to me. After I'd struggled for almost a year to make the wrong relationship work (some head-sick combination of "I've invested too much time" and "What if there's nothing better out there?"), Shane pointed out that I'd be calling him a year from now in exactly the same position (lying fetal in my bed) if I didn't make the break.

That night, in a cab on the way home from a friend's house, I looked over at my boyfriend and decided I was done (it helped that he was head-bobbing drunk—never attractive).

Sometimes, try as we might, we're not meant to be *with* or work *for* the man (watch me turn this into a chapter about entrepreneurship). Sometimes we're meant to go it alone.

Do You Have the Spirit?

To go it alone or not to go it alone? That is the question. Actually the real question is: Are entrepreneurs born or made? This one has been making the rounds for years and there are no definitive answers. I grew up with a dad who's an entrepreneur, so I'm not entirely sure what I was born with and what trickled down from watching him, but I'm going to guess there are more born than made. If you're not born (or able to grow or learn into) what I'm talking about below, you're asking for trouble.

Rules are written for other people. I was speaking at a television industry conference, and before everyone was let into the room, I listened to a guy tell us how hard it is to sell a TV show: "The chances are one in a million." After sharing my story of selling thirteen episodes of a show concept upon first pitch, the guy came up to me and asked how it happened. I didn't say it aloud, but in my mind I'm thinking . . . because I'm not you . . . or the 999,999 others out pitching their show.

It sounds egotistical (and maybe it is), but to be an entrepreneur, you need to believe that the odds, the statistics, and the rules don't apply to you. Nine out of ten start-up businesses fail in the first five years. You'd be fucked walking into this reality and not believe you'll be the one who will defy the odds. This rules-are-for-others concept is also essential from the perspective of looking for new ways of doing things. The name of the game is innovation, and some of the best businesses have been built around taking a tried-and-true idea or rule and turning it on its ass. Rules are not for you.

Fearlessness. Leaving the comfort of the warm, comfortable co-coon of the "man" is not for the faint of heart. As I actually think and write about it here, it's not that as an entrepreneur you don't feel fear—you do—but you become not only im-mune to it, you learn to actually feed off it. If your idea of be-ing out on the limb is ordering pork rather than chicken, you're in for a rude awakening. To put your name, money, reputation on the line is a big, fat, exhilarating deal. You're going to be scared and the question you need to ask yourself is: Can I han-dle it? I've met a lot of failed business owners, and more often than not, they become paralyzed and can't think straight in the face of the fear.

A refusal to lose. I'm not just saying this for the sake of bravado, and it's not that I don't question myself, threaten that I'm leav-ing, or want to give up, but at the end of the day I know I will not let myself lose. And to me that looks like quitting. There's a certain kind of stubbornness that comes with entrepreneur-ship. On the outside it looks like you're crazy to be holding on for dear life, and not giving up at the point at which any other sane, rational person would have bailed. As an entrepreneur you have to be willing to fail (you're going to make mistakes) but you can't let yourself lose—huge difference. One of my very favorite business books is called *Many Miles to Go* by Brian Tracy. His message is one of perseverance and dedication and I use it as a constant reminder that the greater your vision, the longer it will take to build.

The Signs That It's Time

Okay, so you have the spirit and you think you're ready to make the leap. My divorce coincided with my decision to commit to my business and the signs are startlingly similar.

You're giving more than you're getting. You know you're ready to walk out when you're getting so much less than what you're giving and resentment has become your sidekick. You're beyond believing it's ever going to change. I'm all about giving generously to your career, but if you hit a point where it can't give you what you need back, it's time to go. There are so many things we can get from our career in exchange for our efforts, but what I'm talking about here is money. There's a very real point in an employee-employer relationship, particularly in publicly traded companies and government-subsidized industries, where you top out and they can't pay you anthing more.

There are varying formulas out there, depending on the industry and your position, but a company expects your efforts to earn them at least three times (on average) what they are paying you. If you, with your amazing contacts, track record, reputation, are making your company a shitload of cash (five, ten, fifteen times what they're paying you) and they're not willing (or able) to share the wealth, you may want to consider hitting the streets. Sure you're going to be paying your own overhead and health insurance, but run the numbers—you may be better off.

You can't think about anything else. At least for me, I knew it was time when my business moved from passing thought to mild obsession to full-fledged unable to turn it off distraction. When you're at that point of no return, your vision, your idea, your passion for this other business is all-consuming—you're present and accounted for, clocking the hours, but your heart isn't in it. And if you don't leave now, you'll spend the rest of your life regretting the fact that you settled.

There are irreconcilable differences. Some girls aren't meant to be tied down. They hate checking with someone else before they make a decision, they don't want to be told where to be or what to wear, and they're fine with taking full responsibility for both their successes and their failures. If you're just not the type that will ever be content dealing with incompetent colleagues, office politics bullshit, and a career fate that is ultimately in the hands of someone else, it's time to consider the entrepreneurial option.

Trick of the Trade: Cutting the Cord

Before you get all excited and call your boss, make sure you're not thinking:

- **I'm always right**

    Biggest mistake I've seen in entrepreneurs—you think now that you're running your own show, it's all on your terms.

Not even maybe. Now you actually have more cooks in your kitchen—your investor/banker, your clients, your vendors, your freelancers—you've officially never been more wrong.

- **I'll start making money on day one**

Not likely, and even if you do, everything you have will be going back into the business. Have your credit cards, line of credit, friends, and family all lined up and ready to charge.

- **No more assholes**

If only. You've officially entered asshole-central. Now you don't have one boss bugging you, you have as many bosses as you have clients (and let's hope that's a lot).

What You're In For

I'm not joking (or reaching here). Being single and being an entrepreneur have a lot in common. Here's what you can look forward to . . . the good, the bad, and the ugly.

Paying the rent alone

If money is an issue, months before your departure you're going to want to get yourself a little nest egg. No one's going to be writing a check to cover your half of anything for at least a couple of months so get yourself prepared to pay the rent (and tech support, and paper supplies, and FedEx charges, and phone bills).

Time is on your side

When you're in charge of your own schedule, it doesn't matter when you get the job done—your time is spent the way you want to spend it. So if your productivity peak hits at 6 a.m., you don't have to wait around for others to get their asses out of bed before you start your day. Just be sure to be available during normal working hours for those clients who actually work a nine-to-five . . . Suckers!

Garbage duty

Everything you used to ask your assistant (or the cleaning staff) to take care of is officially your domain. Now that everything is riding on your shoulders, you need to be prepared for the degree to which the simple tasks are going to eat into your schedule: like when the photocopier is now eight blocks away.

You work with whom you want to—not whom you have to

Instead of being told that you'll be teaming up with the dick who takes all the credit and can't stop talking about himself, you decide who you're going to hang with—or whether a team of three (you, yourself, and yes, you) is perfect for this particular project.

Lonely nights

No going home (actually no leaving home either) to whine to someone about how bad your day was. Reintroduce yourself to your journal and get used to your own company.

You're the boss

How many times have you sat through unnecessary meetings, committed to projects that you could give two shits about, and given up the work you like doing best just to take one for the team? Now you make the decisions on what to green light, how your strengths are best utilized, what gets priority, and when to delegate. All the remote control reign you ever wanted, and more.

Your call

Getting out of the house is going to take some newfound discipline. Without a time or place to go to, you're going to need to take the initiative, make the call, and book some meetings. Your income and sanity are going to depend upon it. No one's going to know if you haven't made it out of bed this week.

Gather the girls

You're flying solo now and need to find yourself some other single friends. The key to making going it alone work is by surrounding yourself with others in the same boat. Create your own cast of coworkers—people you can brainstorm with, lament to, enforce accountability—just be sure to choose wisely.

It all comes down to you

Being on your own is both scary and exhilarating. Only when you take the leap and walk away are you able to achieve the powerfully freeing realization that you can, in fact, go it alone. Add to that the excitement of bringing a vision of what's possible to life, the notion that you never have to settle, and the knowledge that no one will be able to hold you back from creating the career that's right for you.

Why You Need to Be Willing to Walk Away

Whether you actually do it or not isn't always the point. The power of this rule is in the *willingness*. And the magic of willingness is what happens when it trickles down from your head to your heart. I was divorced for almost three years before I actually became *willing* to leave my husband. I was building my business for almost the same amount of time before I truly became *willing* to share it with a business partner and for it to become a success. The moment you're *willing* to walk away from what's wrong (guy, job, industry) is exactly when you get what WORKS.

Conclusion

You may be too young to remember this, and long before I realized how truly frightening this little tidbit is, feminist author Susan Faludi wrote a book called *Backlash,* which inspired a *Newsweek* article that declared it more likely for a woman to be killed by a terrorist than find herself a husband after the age of 40.

As I near 39 with plenty of suitors and nary a mugger in sight, I can't help but make the connection between the single girl hysteria and the sky-is-falling panic happening in the world of work and call bullshit. Between watching the news and reading the headlines, it's apparently easier to find a man in New York City than a job in finance. As if. But, as you well know by this point in the book, it doesn't matter if you're looking for a man or a job, the lesson is still the same: DON'T BELIEVE THE HYPE. There are a couple of things you need to consider before you start dating David Spade or put your application in at Burger King.

One of the most interesting things that happens in the face of bad news? All the negative Nellys use it as an excuse to give up without even trying. The same way *Newsweek*'s assertion gave women around the country license to dive daily into a pint of Ben and Jerry's (no men around to check out their ass anyway) they simply gave up. I'm not playing Pollyanna here. The unemployment stats are real: people are out of work. And sure, it's taking longer to land a gig than when jobs are flush, but if you're not afraid of some hard work and perseverance you're going to survive. . . . You will, however, need to get off the couch. The majority of your competition is curled up with a bottle of Chardonnay and now's the time to get out there. Your odds have never been better.

And speaking of odds, do you think of yourself as lucky or unlucky? At the end of the day you create your own luck by simply *deciding* you deserve the man, the job, the raise, the promotion. As I write this conclusion, there are 13.2 million people out of work, according to the Department of Labor. But don't stop there. That also means there are 135.7 million people "in" work. What camp do you want to live in—lucky or unlucky? Oh, and keep in mind, *Newsweek* was wrong. The majority of women referred to in the article actually did find a mate without getting car bombed. Wouldn't it be horrifying to look back and realize you didn't apply for the job (or search for the man) of your dreams because you were led to believe you couldn't?

Couldn't, shouldn't, can't—wipe these words from your vocabulary. In fact, every single time you read a statistic or hear someone say you can't, I want it to inspire you to figure out exactly how you can. You are not a statistic. You are not one of the masses. You are a Girl on Top.

Jericho Public Library
1 Merry Lane
Jericho, New York 11753
Phone: 935-6790

GAYLORD